Praise for Maximum

"Sometimes science needs to be bro[ken into] chunks to sustain our wellbeing and encourage growth. Aleks Srbinoski's practical guidance in this book "Maximum Mental Health" does just that. The skills and perspective provided could take upwards of 20 sessions to cover if you were completing individual therapy. My advice, read Aleks' words, let them permeate, and then be active and chip away at the concepts and skills over the next few months. Aleks presents you with tools for change, let them work for you."

Dr. Benjamin L. Wilkes, Clinical Psychologist and Allied Health Manager, Macquarie University.

"An excellent resource on tried-and-tested ideas and techniques to achieve success and maintain full mental health."

Tom Butler-Bowdon, bestselling author of 50 Psychology Classics, 50 Self-Help Classics.

"The author applies evidence-based scientific practice in an accessible and engaging manner that helps the reader overcome one of the most change limiting aspects of ill mental health… motivation. His Fast Action Techniques are the most beneficial aspect as they allow the reader to experience immediate feedback from small and progressive changes in multiple aspects of their life – from work and exercise to relationships and spirituality. Most importantly, the author reminds the reader to get in touch with their Human and participate in that essential human aspect of empathy via compassionate giving. Highly recommended reading."

Dr. Robert A. Battisti, PhD., Principal Clinical Psychologist, Mind Plasticity

"The material in this book is excellent. I commend it highly."

Richard Koch, author of the million-copy bestseller, The 80/20 Principle.

"Is it possible to attain superior mental health? Aleks Srbinoski, clinical psychologist and author of Maximum Mental Health, would answer with a resounding "Yes." In entertaining and highly-readable language, Aleks offers 20 simple but powerful principles for happier and healthier living. I'm not a fan of quick-fix formulas for improving your life. Aleks, however, provides excellent advice based on years of clinical experience and wide reading of the research literature. If you put into practice just a few of the principles in this book, it could change your life."

Dr. Frank Bonkowski, Happiness after midlife and English Communication Specialist.

"The message is clear: No matter the circumstances, you can make simple and fast changes to improve your mental health. Filled with practical strategies that will change lives!"

John G. Miller, bestselling author of QBQ: The Question Behind the Question.

"In a very practical and real way, Aleks Srbinoski's Maximum Mental Health truly leads the reader to maximize his/her own mental health and well-being. As a counselor-turned-mental-health-writer, I'm impressed by the way Srbinoski presents useful information and tools in a way that allows people to both understand and apply the techniques to enhance their mental wellness both immediately and in the long term."

Tanya J. Peterson, Mental Health Columnist and author of critically acclaimed and award-winning mental-health-themed novels.

"What I like the most about Aleks is that he hits the issues head on, then he gives you a big enough reason to change and most impressively, he provides a logical and inspirational path to get the results you want. Most people making big claims seem to cover one aspect of this process, Aleks covers the lot and he delivers – BIG TIME. If you're serious about achieving you own success and happiness, so is Aleks."

Andrew Griffiths, bestselling author of The Me Myth.

"I am the principle and one of the 9 doctors working in a group General Practice. For almost a decade we have been referring our patients struggling with mental illness to Aleks. I have been most impressed with his results, which are confirmed by the feedback from my patients. Now with "Maximum Mental Health", he finally shares all his key principles and secrets so he can help even more people."

Dr. John Cheung, Principle Doctor of Crown West Medical, Registrar Supervisor and Senior Clinical Lecturer

Maximum Mental Health

Also by Aleks George Srbinoski

Happiness Up Stress Down: Increase Happiness and Decrease Stress in just 2 Minutes a Day over 2 Weeks and Help your Community

Destiny Defining Decisions: Best-Selling Entrepreneurs Reveal their Greatest Success Secrets

60 Minute Success Secrets Series Books

Motivation Now

Instant Inner Calm

10 Life Success Secrets Revealed

Precision Language

The 7 Mental Viruses Crushing Your Potential

To be released in 2015

More books from the "Mental Health and Happiness" series

Books can be found on Amazon or mass copies directly sought from the author.

Maximum Mental Health

Overcome Depression, Anxiety and other Mental Illnesses with 20 Principles for Happier and Healthier Living

Aleks George Srbinoski

FULFILLING HAPPINESS PUBLISHING

Disclaimer

The author, contributors and publisher shall have neither liability nor responsibility to any person or entity with respect to any of the information, strategies or exercises contained in this document. The user assumes all risk for any injury, loss or damage caused or alleged to be caused, directly or indirectly by using any information, strategies or exercises described in the "Maximum Mental Health" book and related "Mental Health Hypnosis" materials. All information is generalist in nature. Should any reader make use of information contained herein, this is their decision, and the contributors (and their companies), authors and publishers do not assume any responsibilities whatsoever under any circumstances or conditions.

Copyright

Copyright © 2015 by Aleks George Srbinoski. All rights reserved. No part of this publication may be reproduced, stored in a retrieval system, or transmitted in any form or by any means, photocopying, mechanical, electronic, recording or otherwise; without the prior written consent from the publisher.

1st ed.

ISBN 978-0-9925826-2-3

For my father who always told me to "keep going." I will!

Acknowledgements

Thank you to all my past psychology related teachers, supervisors and accreditors. Even the ones I didn't always agree with.

To my Dutchess, you are my true north and always the greatest source of assistance.

To my family, thanks to you, "little Aleks" might actually be growing up!

As for all my friends and clients of the past, present and future, may the inspiration I draw from our encounters return to you tenfold.

Contents

Introduction 1
How to Best Use this Book 8

Part 1: The Principles of Increasing Motivation 10

Behavior is King 11
Control Your Environment or It Will Control You 16
Move to Find Your Groove 21
Positive Focus 27
Mindful Acceptance 32

Part 2: The Principles of Enhancing Mood and Living Well 40

Pure Pleasures 41
A Real and Supportive Social Life 47
Optimism Wins 54
New-You Nutrition 60
Deep Sound Sleep 68

Part 3: The Principles of Meaningful Living 74

Expose Yourself to Overcome Fear and Anxiety 75
Cycles of Life 82
Praise Pays 89
Gratitude 97
Meaning 105

Part 4: The Principles of Life Mastery 112

Authentic Achievement 113
Easy Goal Setting and Accountability 121
Valuable Living 128
Peak Performance 137
Sensational Self Image 145
Your Two Bonus Chapters 154

Bonus: Principles of Magnetism 155
    Harmonious Relationships 156
    Superior Social Skills 164
    Medication 172
    Dealing with Extreme Situations 174
    Seeking Professional Assistance 176
    Personal Bibliography and Research References 178

Introduction

Seeking a Cure through the 4 Ms of Superior Mental Health

Thank you for obtaining a copy of this book. I am Aleks George Srbinoski (Aleks George for short), Australian life coach and hypnotherapist. Most importantly, in relation to this book, I am a fully trained Clinical Psychologist with over a decade of one-on-one therapeutic experience. In my years as a Clinical Psychologist, I've worked with a great number of people and helped them overcome countless varieties of problems.

One of the key secrets to life success is to work to understand the core principles underlying happiness and superior mental health. There are thousands of techniques designed to assist someone overcome depression, anxiety and other psychological issues. However, no technique is ever 100% foolproof or applicable 100% of the time. The best way to overcome an issue is to understand the life principle that lies underneath the problem. By uncovering and understanding the principle, in time you will be able to create your own techniques to help you solve your own specific problems. Rest assured, I have added key techniques for you as well until you are able to develop your own.

Understanding the principles rather than just strategies or techniques is the key to masterful learning in any field. My goal is for you to develop a deep understanding of what is required to live a happy and mentally healthy life. To do this, I have gone through every book and program I have ever created as well as reflected on the most common problems and solutions created in all my years as a therapist. From all that research, I was able to distil everything I know into 20 core principles to help people not just overcome depression, anxiety and other common life issues, but also live a happy, healthy and meaningful life.

The 4 Ms of Mental Health

The 20 principles have been placed into four categories. Although you do not need to read this book chronologically and can simply choose whatever is most appropriate for you to work through at any point, each principle and category does build on the previous.

The four categories are:
- Motivation
- Mood
- Meaning
- Mastery

The first set of principles are motivational, and designed to get you active and moving in the right direction as quickly as possible. The next set is focused on enhancing mood and feeling well. Following this, you learn how to overcome fear and develop deeper and more empowering meaning. Finally, the keys to achieving life mastery are outlined. As a bonus, I also added two additional social principles to be revealed at the end. These focus on the skills required for being highly influential and positively magnetic in your close relationships and in more social situations. Consider magnetism the fifth M if you like.

Curing Anxiety and Depression

Can this book actually help you cure anxiety or depression? The answer is it is definitely possible. Legally, I cannot state that my methods will or have led to a cure as anxiety and mood fluctuations are part of the human condition and new life events could lead to a re-occurrence of symptoms. What I will officially say is my methods have assisted many people overcome clinical anxiety and depression symptoms and remain without clinical symptoms in the long term. To achieve mental health depends on a range of factors, two in particular. One is your level of commitment and the second is the severity of the problem. If you do not apply the principles, then they will not work for you. The severity of your symptoms will also determine your ability in applying these principles. Someone who is severely anxious or depressed may actually struggle to concentrate and read, so that would obviously make using this book correctly much more difficult.

As a general rule, if you have mild to moderate levels of depression or anxiety, applying the principles in this book could be enough for you to overcome the problem. I have many examples where I have simply educated a client on one or two of these principles and it was enough for them to overcome their depression or anxiety issue.

However, these of course, were not severe cases. In severe cases, I would still utilize the key principles offered in this book but usually in combination with additional techniques and hypnotic interventions. In even more extreme cases, I would enlist the assistance of other professionals such as psychiatrists and other medical and health practitioners.

It is helpful to start with a general guide of how you are at present in terms of Depression, Anxiety and Stress. The best starting point is to examine yourself with a psychological scale called the DASS21. A simple online search will point you to the scale and it is easy to score. It will tell you if you are currently fine (in the Normal range) or if your symptoms are Mild, Moderate, Severe or Extremely Severe. If severe or extremely severe, it may be wise to visit your family doctor for a formal mental health evaluation. I have outlined at the end of this book under what conditions seeking additional assistance may be warranted.

For someone who is *in the "normal" range and more self-improvement focused; or who is suffering from only mild to moderate range issues*, the application of these principles alone can and often is enough to become happier and healthier and overcome a range of mental health issues. I will also provide links to additional books I have written if you would like more information on a particular topic area and links to hypnotic interventions if you are seeking additional assistance in relation to a certain area of life. (Hypnotic interventions tend to be faster and more thorough as I can guide you better with my voice – more on this in a moment.) The principles in this book in combination with hypnotic re-training can and often do create fantastic results for the people I counsel.

There is Nothing Hypnotic in this Book

There is <u>no hypnosis</u> and <u>nothing hypnotic</u> in this book. This is a book of psychological principles and techniques. Psychology and hypnosis although complimentary, are two different disciplines. However, there are links at the end of each chapter to specialized hypnotic recordings if you feel they may be of use.

I'll explain why I have added these options in a moment. First, let me state, you will not need to obtain any of my other books or hypnotic recordings to make the most of this book. I have done my best to give you all the essential elements required for superior mental health. As you will see, I have not held anything back. The reason I have added optional links to additional hypnotic recordings is to increase the speed and ease of your success. Use these options only if they are right for you.

Differences between Psychological and Hypnotic Intervention

To understand the differences, it helps to first understand how we learn. Your mind can be separated into two parts. There is the conscious mind and the unconscious (or sometimes referred to as the subconscious) mind. The conscious mind relates to what you are currently aware of at any one time (which for most people is only between 5-9 elements of your experience) whilst your unconscious mind is helping you to take care of thousands of activities without your awareness.

Your unconscious mind is what makes your heart beat, your wounds heal, your senses to work and operates your major habits (good and bad) automatically. Most habits are outside your conscious awareness. When you learn anything new, you first learn it unconsciously and you do not always recognize what you have learnt consciously. This is why people often don't know why they do what they do or how often they do it. It may have to be brought to their conscious attention by someone else or by consciously using psychological methods to recognize and measure the size of the habit.

Psychological intervention works by building your conscious awareness of what the problem is and how you can change it by learning new techniques to overcome the problem. By consciously and consistently practicing those new techniques, over time the unconscious mind will accept the new practice and it will become a new unconscious habit. Psychological methods work by consciously training a new skill until it is accepted by the unconscious and becomes a habit.

Psychological intervention offered by an established professional is the most scientifically tested and proven method for increasing happiness and overcoming anxiety and depression issues. A Clinical Psychologist must have a minimum of six years of university training before qualification.

Hypnosis is a different discipline and works by specifically instructing the unconscious mind to change the habit. By directly instructing the unconscious mind to make the required changes, positive improvement is often much faster. It is not uncommon for me to assist someone in overcoming a debilitating issue or habit via hypnosis in as little as 15-20 minutes. Of course, a person with multiple and severe issues cannot be assisted in just 20 minutes. Hypnosis works best by changing one specific habit at a time.

However, hypnosis is not for everyone. Although everyone is hypnotizable, not everyone is open to the process. Some people for whatever reason simply do not want to be hypnotized. The most common reason is some people do not like the idea of having little control over a mental change process. Hypnosis works best when people stop analyzing, relax and trust in the process. Not everyone is willing to do that and so purely psychological technique training is best for such people. Ironically, most of the time it is overly controlling and analytical person that would benefit from hypnosis the most.

There are also many myths and misconceptions about hypnosis. If working with a skilled therapist, it is not dangerous, you cannot get stuck in it and you can choose to come out of it at any time. Unfortunately, unlike Clinical Psychology with its extensive history of scientific testing that support the core principles you will discover in this book, hypnosis does not have the same stringent level of scientific testing behind it. There are also many deeply unskilled practicing hypnotists.

Unlike the minimum six years required to become a Clinical Psychologist, you can call yourself a hypnotist and start offering therapy to people after completing a weekend course. This happens often and the results, as you can imagine are usually very disappointing. Finding a skilled hypnotherapist with the proper training and a deep understanding of the human mind and of mental health and mental illness is rare. I have studied and analyzed many of the leading psychologists in the world and have been trained by some of the best hypnotists.

Your Experiential Gifts – Mindfulness and Hypnosis Recordings

It helps to actually be guided when re-training the mind. As you will discover, developing the mental skill of mindfulness will be an important part of this book. Although I do outline how to do it yourself, it is easier to be guided through the experience.

In order to assist you, I have made three mindfulness recordings available to you for free. They are taken from my Fulfilling Happiness program which is a highly exclusive and comprehensive life coaching program designed to help people achieve true meaningful happiness and avoid depression, anxiety, anger and other debilitating life problems. It took me over two years to create the program and to date, has never been publicly released. It is only available by special request to the people who qualify for it and agree to sign a confidentiality agreement.

You will be able to download and listen to the recordings whenever you like. As an additional gift, I have also added a complete hypnosis recording. Do you feel like you could use a break or have a holiday? The recording I have added will allow you to feel all the relaxing and rejuvenating benefits of having had an amazing 7 day holiday experience in less than 35 minutes. It's called **"The Ultimate Beach Island Holiday Escape."**

Most people have never experienced hypnosis. The vast majority that do, if conducted by a skilled therapist, find hypnosis to be a highly enjoyable and greatly beneficial process. Combined psychological and hypnotic interventions complement each other extremely well if utilized correctly. I thought it would be useful should you become interested in pursuing hypnotic options that you have a complete sample of it first. To obtain access to your free mindfulness and hypnosis recordings, go now to the site http://MentalHealthHypnosis.com

Enjoy your gifts and get ready for journey ahead,

Aleks

How to Best Use this Book

You are about to discover the 20 core principles for greater happiness and health. I have worked to address all the major areas of life: *motivation, nutrition, exercise, sleep, pleasure, achievement, confidence, relationships, overcoming fears and anxiety, improving mood and self-image, getting past setbacks and grief, developing optimism, meaningful living and so on.*

You may not be interested in all of these areas at this time. Although preferred, you do not need to read this book chronologically. You can focus on the chapters and principles most relevant to you now. It is important not to try and do too much too soon. You can always go back and work on additional principles once you have worked through your most pressing issues.

Future Additions

This book will help you but is also general in nature. Some people will benefit from additional help in relation to specific mental health issues. For example, there are many forms of anxiety (phobias, social, panic, OCD, trauma) and someone in the severe range category of one of these issues may benefit from more specialized assistance.

Therefore, based on demand, I may in the future use the principles you are about to discover again to address more specific mental health issues such as particular types of anxiety, depression and addictions. Regardless of the severity of your issues, the following principles if applied will assist you and quite possibly lead to a great result if issues are not too severe.

Special Note: I have also outlined what to do at the end of this book if you feel you may require additional assistance for a severe problem. You can still use the principles of this book and any (optional) hypnotic recordings to assist you whilst seeking personalized help if needed.

If you are unsure, you can always email me any time at aleks@fulfillinghappiness.com I am highly responsive and should be able to point you in the right direction. I can answer any general questions you have. I cannot offer therapy via email (see the end of this book for options) and **DO NOT CONTACT ME IF IT IS AN EMERGENCY!** See the final chapters, "Dealing with Extreme Situations" and "Seeking Professional Assistance" if unsure of what to do in an emergency.

What is most important is that you are safe and always have the right level of assistance available to you. I think that is enough discussion of precautions. There will be more key precautionary advice at the end.

It is now time to develop yourself and have some fun.

Enjoy discovering and applying the following principles.

Part 1: The Principles of Increasing Motivation

Behavior is King
Revealing the Secret of Motivation Psychology

You are not what you think! You are not what you feel. You become what you do. Human psychology is often broken up into three simple components: thoughts, feelings and behavior.

I believe the way you should judge yourself and your life is exactly the same way a court of law would judge you. A court of law does not care what you think; it does not care what you feel. The only thing that matters when it comes to true judgment is … what did you do?

Imagine you are walking down the street, (I assume this to be a frequent fantasy of most postal workers) and suddenly a small and highly irritating dog catches you off guard and barks aggressively at you. Instantly you feel a surge of anger. You imagine kicking the dog so it shuts up and whimpers away never to bother you again.

Are you a bad person for thinking that way? Are you an aggressive person for feeling angry? Let's put the matter in front of the judge.

The judge hears the story and asks …

Judge: What did you then do?

You: Nothing.

Judge: Then you're free to go. Case dismissed.

A court can only judge you on what you do. It does not matter what you think and feel until those thoughts and feelings lead to a particular action. It is your behavior that will either reinforce and strengthen or reduce and weaken a set of thoughts and feelings.

If you followed the urge to kick the dog and tried doing so, or even succeeded at kicking it, then the next time you're in a similar situation you are more likely to think and feel and do the same thing again. Those thoughts and feelings will intensify with each behavioral repetition. If on the other hand you did nothing, you are likely to have less of those thoughts and feelings, and they would be less intense, if a similar scenario was to occur again. This would also free up your mind to find other ways of coping with the situation, such as calming yourself and finding alternatives to deal with the dog like speaking to its owner, distracting it or avoiding it in the future.

What we are looking at is human motivation. What makes you do what you do? More importantly, how can you make the right decisions and live your best life, even when tempted otherwise?

To compel you to do the right thing and increase your motivation, it will help if I first put on my 'practical philosopher/psychologist' hat and reveal to you what I believe are the most powerful concepts you need to understand in order to be a successful human being.

There are four concepts (which can each be explained with one word only) that you need to understand in order to maximize your motivation and make the right choices. What do you think is the most important word in human language? Take a moment to really think about it. The answer is about to be revealed right …

NOW! (Variations include: instant, immediate, etc.)

In my opinion, "now" must be the most important word there is. There is only now! The past is gone, the future hasn't happened yet. The only thing that matters is now.

The second most important word is…

ACT! (Variations include: do, behave, etc.)

These two words put together, NOW ACT or ACT NOW, are the most powerful and motivating force on the planet. The final words are also very important, but unlike what many believe and feel, I think they are not as powerful as "now" and "act."

The third word is…

BELIEF! (Variations include: be, think, perceive, attitude, etc.)

Behavior is King 13

The fourth word is ...

EMOTION! (Variations include: feeling, sense, etc.)

Many people probably consider belief to be the most important. I don't believe so! Let's try an experiment. Stand up and walk over to the other side of the room, touch the wall, and then walk back to your starting position. Do the same thing another two times. As you do this say out loud and believe and feel as much as you can: "I can't walk to that wall, touch it and come back. I can't walk to that wall touch it and come back etc."

Could you do it? Absolutely you could! Because you can ACT NOW in a way that opposes what you are feeling, thinking, saying and believing. Now the 'wise guy or gal' might say, "yeah but part of me must have believed I could do it in order to do it." Maybe, and that is why developing empowering thoughts and feelings will also be covered. But, let me ask you this ...

Have you ever truly and honestly felt and believed one thing (e.g. "I am going to fail this test, I feel sick, there is no point in doing it") but despite believing it acted anyway (e.g. did the test) and had a successful outcome?

That is because your beliefs will change not based on what you think but on what you do now! You cannot lie to yourself. At the end of the day, what you do will change your life, but what you feel and think will not, unless you act on it now.

So how does this all this relate to mental health? Many people believe that they have to be feeling positive and motivated to begin and succeed at a task. Absolutely wrong!

Motivation often comes during the task and after the task is completed, not before! This is especially the case if you happen to be feeling depressed, anxious, angry or 'off' in some other kind of way. Decisive action is crucial to success. As you NOW ACT and keep ACTING NOW, that is when the motivation begins to build. As motivation builds, more empowering thoughts and feelings tend to follow too.

Have you ever not felt motivated to go to work, exercise, or go out or anything at all, but you did it anyway? And, the more you did it, the more motivated you started to feel and by the end of it you were feeling really motivated.

Of course! That is because motivation is the reward, not the starting point. All acts require the most effort in the beginning. Starting is the hardest part. When you keep ACTING NOW, it becomes easier, more motivating and more satisfying.

It's like pushing a boulder down a hill. The first big push is the hardest, but once you're rolling it becomes easier and easier. Then when you feel the reward of getting to the bottom of the hill, that's when you feel the most motivated - after it's over.

You need to understand that you will be rewarded with the most motivation and the greatest mental health boost after it's over. That's when your beliefs have caught up to your actions and your brain says, "Wow, I did it, and because I did it, I can now feel really good about it."

Of course, that doesn't mean there aren't ways to develop motivating thoughts and feelings as well. You will be learning them too. The point is you don't have to feel positive and motivated in the beginning to achieve what you want to achieve.

Think of it this way. It will not matter what you think, if you don't act in the way you want to act. Without acting now, your beliefs will lead you nowhere. You will start to develop new disempowering beliefs because you can't lie to yourself. This is why people who use affirmations but do nothing to act on them, become depressed.

There is no motivational philosophy greater than "just do it… NOW!" Positive and motivating beliefs must be conditioned through immediate action. Motivation is a reward for behavior, not thinking. That is why regardless of how big or small the goal, you must always in some way "ACT NOW" towards it despite what you may think or feel.

Principle Summary

Behavior is King: Revealing the secret of motivation psychology.

You can only be judged by what you do. Taking immediate action (no matter how small) is the key to motivation and successful living.

Fast-Action Techniques

1. Consider a task or project you have been putting off. Start it immediately! It doesn't matter if you think you are not ready or if you don't feel like it. It's irrelevant. Do it for at least 10-30 minutes and notice the increase in your motivation afterwards.
2. You can only be judged by what you do. Turn this upcoming statement or one similar into a mantra you repeat to yourself regularly throughout the day, "What I do now is who I am becoming." Do this at least three times at the start of any important task.
3. Choose a task that you loathe but must be done. Take the smallest step you can towards it and see how it is not as bad as you think or feel. Commit to spend just one minute on your taxes, or dishes or whatever else you have been avoiding, and see if you can focus on just one minute at a time. Since the goal was just one minute, everything else will be a bonus and should lead to increasing motivation and better feelings about the task.

Hypnotic Recording – Decisiveness and Fast Action Taking to Get Things Done: For guided assistance in moving beyond the principles and techniques of this chapter, a guided brain retraining process aimed at developing a decisive mind, eliminating procrastination tendencies and being more action orientated and dynamic at work, home and socially is available now at this link – http://mentalhealthhypnosis.com/decisiveness

Control Your Environment or It Will Control You
Be calmer, more creative and find peace the simple way

I often say to people: "why make life harder than it has to be?"

When it comes to problem solving, there are two main methods to make a change. You can change the internal/mental environment or the external/physical environment. Whenever possible, change the external environment first. It's often a lot faster, much easier and may even completely solve the problem.

For example, imagine you are an employer and you have two employees with separate and independent job roles who sit near each other and frequently argue and cause other disruptions. Initial requests for them to stop bickering haven't worked.

One option: Sit them both down, talk through the issue, offer mediation and mental training if necessary in order to discover the core issues and assist them to develop better communication and coping mechanisms.

The other option: Move them to opposite sides of the room or to different floors.

What would you do first? I know what I would do. Since they can't figure out a way to get along, I would tell them to no longer communicate unless necessary and then flip a coin in front of them and move them accordingly.

More times than not, this would completely solve the problem. It wouldn't solve their dislike for each other, but that is not the problem. As long as the work environment is harmonious and people are getting their work done, personal feelings and relationships are not relevant.

It is only if the bickering continues that psychological intervention would need to be explored. However, since you have actively increased the space between the triggers (each other), the opportunity for bickering has been greatly reduced and this may be enough.

Your environment shapes what you do and who you become more than you realize. In over 50% of the population in many major Western countries, people are struggling with high stress and a big part of the reason is because of how busy everyone seems to be. There is so much going on and people are constantly being interrupted and expected to be moving in several directions at the same time.

The phone is ringing, texts are coming, email, chats and social media updates are happening plus there are all those ads everywhere trying to manipulate you too. You also have to deal with all kinds of annoying people, with whom you probably live or work.

Is it easier to feel calmer in a quiet temple or on a busy highway? You might say, "Well, yeah, the temple, but the problem is I seem to live on a busy highway."

Then the question becomes: "How do you make your highway more temple like?"

Based on the ebb and flow of traffic, what tasks are best done at what times and what adjustments can you make? Could you plant some trees on one of the islands in the road? Could you paint parts of it a different color? Could you wear earmuffs during times your safety doesn't depend on you needing to listen? Could you install a more relaxing chair? Could you put in a detour for part of the day? Could you change your attitude or meditate on the noise you hear?

Absolutely you could and the best part is, although it may often feel like it, you don't live in the middle of a highway! What do you need to do to create a better environment at work or home?

Let's begin with the outside and move inwards. How much color is in your environment and where is it located? Different colors trigger different emotions. Blue is the color that triggers calmness the most. Green also is associated with nature and tends to lead to more peacefulness. Could you add a little more soothing blue or green in your environment?

I am not suggesting you go and paint everything blue and green. You don't always want to be calm, but having something to focus on that is blue or green may help. This leads me to my next point.

What kind of images are in your environment? Do you have images, pictures, paintings and quotes that represent and inspire the right feelings? Oxygen is also essential to feeling good and being more productive. Could you have more plants, or open more windows?

Anything that is symbolic of a calm and creative environment in the external world will trigger more creativity and calmness in your mind. Use natural light if possible. What are the natural smells you enjoy (many people say lavender is calming) and can you add a new scent to your environment? Water is calming and some people have little fountains in certain places. Could you use different fabrics and could you lightly play whatever music that calms you? Cater to your five senses!

All you need to do is simply add the things that naturally make you feel calmer. Adding things that cater to your natural senses is one thing but subtracting the distractions is much, much more important. Simply stated…

KILL THE CLUTTER BEFORE IT KILLS YOU!

Clutter may not actually kill you physically, but it will increase distraction and kill your natural creativity, focus and clarity. Cleanliness, or at least the perception of it, also increases the value of an item or even a person. A well-groomed person is seen to be more interesting, intelligent and attractive. If you go to purchase a home, the owner, if they are intelligent, will at the very least tidy the home and clean it. Some very minor renovations can also often lead to a large increase in value.

If you were to enter the home and be distracted by clutter or dirt, you will associate clutter and dirt with the home whether you want to or not. If it is clean and tidy, your mind is free to start imagining with greater ease what you could add to it to make it your own. The external environment becomes symbolic of your internal environment.

Consider this for a few moments. Imagine a really cluttered room and notice how you feel: heavy, distracted and unfocused.

Now, imagine a tidy room and what do you feel? Light, clear-headed and focused.

Envision your dream home or workplace. Do you envision rooms filled with papers, clothes, food, buzzing devices and other junk all over the place?

NO YOU DON'T!

Not even Obsessive Compulsive Hoarders imagine rooms full of junk. In fact, it's just the opposite, they dream of being able to start again with an uncluttered and calming environment. Unfortunately, the confusing symbolic meaning they have attached to all the junk, which they don't need, makes it incredibly difficult for them to let go of it.

Because of this, they struggle to feel good and to find their natural creativity and focus. What you need to do now is quite simple. Tidy up the spaces where you spend most of your time and most importantly, **MAINTAIN IT.**

Do a short sweep of your environment each morning, especially your work area, and get everything that is not immediately relevant in order and out of sight. This includes switching off and removing irrelevant devices and apps. Keep your area tidy so you can specifically focus on each task at hand. Clean up and organize any distracting files on your computer (e.g. the files on your desktop).

Also study ergonomics, get a good chair, table, and maintain proper posture. With all these external modifications, you are going to feel less fatigue and irritations, higher energy and more natural focus, clarity and calm. Finally, aim to spend more time outside. Nothing clears the mind like a short walk, especially if it is in a naturally green setting.

Although having naturally calming and inspiring objects in your internal environment does help, it does not have the same effect as the real thing. Your mind can enjoy and connect to the symbol to improve mood but it will not be fooled. Going outside every day and spending time in real nature (with your gadgets off) is essential for good mental health.

Principle Summary

Control Your Environment or It Will Control You: Be calmer, more creative and find peace the simple way.

Your environment influences and shapes your mood, creativity and attitudes. A clear and clutter free environment will tend to inspire a clear, creative and clutter free mind. It is easier and often possible to solve a problem through a simple environmental change alone.

Fast-Action Techniques

1. Make a list of all the maintainable ways you could improve your work and home environment on a daily basis. Change just one small habit at a time and only move on to the next one after you are sure you can maintain the newly implemented habit.
2. Set up periods in your day that is device and distraction free. A short distraction free walk in nature each day is a must. Even five minutes will help greatly, though 20 minutes or more is ideal.
3. Consider the people who make up your usual environments and how you can spend more or less time with them depending on your goals. Start with the most distracting or irritating person and think of how you could reduce your time with them.

Hypnotic Recording – Creating Inspiring Environments and Habits: For guided assistance in moving beyond the principles and techniques of this chapter, a guided brain re-training process aimed at making calming and creative environmental changes and developing smarter habits is available now at the link http://mentalhealthhypnosis.com/environment

Move to Find Your Groove
Develop self-confidence, exercise motivation and mental fitness by increasing movement

You know you've met this kid. You've probably met dozens if not hundreds of them. The kid might even live with you. This kid can make you feel young, even if you're not. Everything he or she does is done with full physical commitment. When he runs, he sprints as hard as he can. When she dances, it is wild and free and when they smile, every muscle in their face is stretched to its maximum. Could this be one of their secrets to happiness?

I previously stated that when you "act now", your motivation immediately begins to increase. By definition, an act requires some form of movement. Like the boulder down the hill, the more you start moving, the more motivating momentum you begin to build.

If this is the case, then is it safe to assume that the more expressive and dynamic you are in your movement, the more motivated you will feel? Yes! Let's play a game, if you have encountered some of my work before you may have played this game already, but let's do it again just for fun.

Think of a depressed person and answer ...

Is their head up or down, eyes forward or down, breathing full or shallow, shoulders back or slumped, feeling heavy or light, showing a little or a lot of facial expression, generally have positive, expansive and creative thoughts or negative, critical and restricting thoughts?

Now think of someone who is confident, happy and motivated. You get the opposite answers don't you? This person has their head up, eyes forward, shoulders back, breathing full, feeling light, shows a lot of facial expression and has expansive and creative thoughts.

What is the obvious difference between the two? The confident, happy, motivated person is more dynamic, more expressive: in simple terms they generate energy, positive emotion and motivation through movement.

Obesity related illnesses are the biggest health problems on the planet and guess what the second biggest problem will be within the decade: Depression. You think they are both connected? Absolutely! What do the obese and the depressed share in common? Neither of them moves very much.

In relation to these health problems there are of course many people on medication, and depending on the damage done, they may be recommended. What you may not know is no drug can create new chemicals in your body. They can only interact with the chemicals already there. This is important because there is more than one way to change the interactions and flow of chemicals in your body. A drug is one way to do it, often with troubling side effects.

The fastest natural way to increase the flow of the "happy" chemicals in your body is through dynamic movement. Try it now, create the biggest smile you can (engage your whole face), hold it and notice the sudden happy chemical rush ... Now soften your eyes and make a slow, long, wide, calming smile and feel instantly calm.

The more you move, the greater the flow of serotonin, noradrenaline, dopamine and endorphins through the body, and especially to the brain. The first three are your classic "happy" chemicals, while endorphins also increase the pleasure you feel and at the same time act as natural pain killers or tranquilisers (notice the word - TRANQUIL-isers).

Endorphins increase pleasure and induce calmness and you can maximize their effect by MOVING! To live a tasty life, think of it this way. In a bottle of orange juice, it is the pulp that carries most of the flavor and nutrients. When you first get a bottle of orange juice, where is the pulp?

Sitting at the bottom, right? To make the juice taste good and to absorb the nutrients, what to do you have to do? You shake it up! You set it up so the key nutrients circulate and flow.

Laughing feels great because it involves so much of your body, so does sex and, of course, exercise. Exercise is the ultimate natural regular "happy and calming" chemical creator. You generally don't feel calm during it because you are moving too quickly, but a short time after you've finished and you have your breath back ...

Now you get to feel the euphoria and deep sense of calmness, and although the effects taper off over time, they do last the entire day! So, how do you use the movement principle to your motivational advantage? Before you set yourself to do a task, you always want to warm yourself up and get the motivation flowing by moving in some graded dynamic way.

You want to move towards being highly dynamic but you don't start off that way immediately. You need to build it. Let me explain through a highly physical example first and then we will move on to mildly physical tasks. Let's say you have decided to go for a run first thing in the morning. Of course, even if you don't feel motivated at first, you will NOW ACT on that goal anyway because you know the motivation will come and it will be worth it.

That being said, you don't start at 100%. In other words, as soon as you wake up, you shouldn't leap out of bed, head out to the street and start sprinting. You will hurt yourself and potentially look kind of crazy as you probably should have taken a little bit more time to put some clothes on!

Jokes aside, what you need to do is build up your dynamic movement. You should probably start with some light stretches, moving on to some more dynamic stretches and follow with a light jog. As those chemicals and your motivation begin to flow, you can then start to increase the intensity of what you are doing.

Pretty simple, when it comes to a highly physical example, isn't it? It's actually not any different when it comes to only mildly physical tasks. What do I mean by mildly physical? I mean the kind of tasks and jobs the majority of the world spend most of their time doing these days. I think it is safe to say that most people spend the majority of their working day sitting and moving very little.

This can and is a very big problem because motivation and energy come from movement. Then what do you need to do? The answer is the same as the highly physical example. You need to warm up in a graded and dynamic way.

I can hear you say: "Warm up to sit down and use a computer all day! How does that work?" The exact same way. Before you sit down to begin the task, spend 30 seconds or so stretching your body and then move into giving your body a bit of a vibrant shake. Straighten your posture and begin to breathe more deeply. Then say something positive and encouraging to yourself, sit in a straight active posture and begin.

Don't worry if you don't understand what I mean about saying something positive and encouraging to yourself, you will learn all about that a little later. This way, your body has been activated for work. By moving dynamically, you have just sent a rush of 'happy and motivating' chemicals to your brain. This way, it's easier to begin and beginning is the hardest part.

The effects of course will not last all day. That's why you need to do it often. You need to train yourself so that whenever you start to feel and become less dynamic, you get up, have a quick stretch and a vibrant shake out, straighten your posture, begin breathing deeply and then sit back down to work. This whole process can take less than 30 seconds!

Of course, you can add to it if you like. The more you move, the better you feel. You can put on a song and dance for a few minutes, shadow box, jump up and down or give yourself or get someone else to give you a quick massage. All these actions get those happy and motivating chemicals flowing back to the brain.

To put it simply: whenever you slump, get up! Practice doing this often. A 30 second stretch and move every 15-60 minutes depending on how you are feeling is going to save you hours of time in otherwise slumped over lost productivity. In fact, it has become such a motivating process for me now, that the more creative and productive I begin to feel the more I want to move and feel the flow. I usually stay in my chair but I still enjoy moving as I'm in it. That is the power of movement.

As you will discover, dynamic movement does not just increase your energy and effectiveness, it positively influences others as well and changes the way they view you. All great acts in life require dynamic action. The more free and open you are in your expression, the better you will feel and the more you will achieve.

Principle Summary

Move to Find Your Groove: Develop self-confidence, exercise motivation and mental fitness by increasing movement.

The more you move (in every way) the better you feel. Movement (and of course the most intense version of it - exercise) allows the "happy chemicals" to flow more completely through your mind and body.

Fast-Action Techniques

1. At an absolute minimum, you should be exercising for 20-30 minutes 3-4 times a week. To improve fitness, you can increase the duration and/or the intensity of the routine. Since most people are time poor, regular increases in intensity is more sustainable. In terms of cardiovascular exercise (walking, running, aerobics, etc.), increasing intensity would involve extending periods of higher speed (e.g. power walks or sprints) within your workout. In terms of weight training, it would be increasing the weight and/or reducing the rest periods between exercises. Assuming you are medically able, the greater the intensity, the better the results. More exercise and being more dynamic in general during the day are also likely to assist you in sleeping better at night.

2. Set a timer and set it to ring every 60 minutes. Whenever it rings, spend 30 seconds to a minute stretching and breathing deeply and then adjusting your posture and facial expression before returning to your task. Another option if possible is to vigorously exercise for just 1-2 minutes. Do as many push ups, or sit ups, or star jumps as you can in that period. You will feel very energetic afterwards and you would not have been exercising long enough to have become sweaty.

3. Before important meetings with others, consider how you could be more dynamic and expressive and adjust your physiology accordingly. You will have better control of what occurs and be seen as more confident and positive.

Hypnotic Recording – Increasing Energy and Exercise Motivation: For guided assistance in moving beyond the principles and techniques of this chapter, a guided brain re-training process to assist you in becoming increasingly energetic and expressive as well as more motivated to enjoyably exercise safely and with progressive intensity for greater health and strength is at this link - http://mentalhealthhypnosis.com/energyandexercise

Positive Focus
Learn the simplest and most effective positive thinking habit

Imagine being in the jungle. As you move through it, you notice something out the corner of your eye that captures your attention with a whooshing sound. You proceed cautiously and find yourself at a beautiful clearing. There is a majestic waterfall, surrounded by stunning greenery. The air is crisp, and the mix of wild scents is soothing. To your bafflement, you start to hear singing. The voice is powerful and melodic. You track the sound to under the waterfall and then your pupils dilate and your heart starts racing before you even realize it.

You're intoxicated by what you see, surely the most beautiful person you have ever come across. The person is freely swimming under the waterfall and just so happens to be naked! You are seen but rather than retreating, the person looks at you with eyes of desire and signals you to join. You smile and eagerly step forward but then you suddenly hear a tiger growl. Where does your attention go?

At the most basic level of life, we are driven by two things. **Avoid pain and seek pleasure.** That's it! Anytime you do anything, it's because of one or both of those things. However, one drive is stronger than the other. Is it the beautiful person or the tiger that arrests your attention? **The number one rule of life is PROTECT YOURSELF! Avoid pain as much as possible.** However, a conditioned focus on pain avoidance is not necessary and is less likely to lead to success.

Knowing that the stronger natural drive is to avoid pain, how does that shape our psychology? Take a moment now to consider this scenario. You're a learner racing car driver. You are racing along and about to enter a sharp corner. On the edge of that corner is a very large wall and you are driving a very expensive car at high speed. What do you think as you move into that corner?

Most people when I ask them this say "don't hit the wall!" That is a great idea, but a stupid piece of advice. By thinking about the wall, and not hitting the wall, and how expensive the car is, and how bad it would be if you were to hit the wall and how they're shouldn't be a wall there in the first place, where is your attention? **ON THE WALL!**

Where your attention goes, energy flows. Even though you are trying to avoid it, by putting so much energy on the wall, you are actually more likely to hit it. Crazy, but true. Just like if you are in pain and you angrily focus on that pain and how much you hate it, you will feel it even more. Before I explain what is going on, I'm going to ask you a few questions.

>Would you rather be:
>>Less Stressed or More Relaxed?
>>Less Anxious or More Confident?
>>Less Fat or More Trim?

If you think these are trick questions, you would almost be right. If you examine these questions, they seem to be asking the same thing. If you are less stressed, you would be more relaxed. If you are less anxious, you would be more confident. If you are less fat, you would be more trim. Logically, they appear to be asking the same thing and therefore your answer should not matter. Except it does!

One of the biggest mistakes people make is they assume people are generally logical and rational. Wrong! People are primarily emotional. Although we have the ability to be rational, it is not how we naturally exist.

When we receive information, it is first processed at the instinctual level (will this be painful and should I avoid it or will this be pleasurable and should I move towards it). Then we examine at the emotional level (how does this make me feel) and only then, if the information has not been acted on at the first two levels, would you consider "what does this mean rationally?" Most of the information you perceive does not get to that level of processing.

Let's explore, "less fat or more trim." If you had a computer for a brain, it would not matter. If you are less fat, you are trimmer and if you are trimmer you are less fat. Now say out loud "I want to be less fat" versus "I want to be more trim." Say them again and notice how it feels.

If you achieve the goal of becoming less FAT, what are you? You are still fat! Your overall perception of the kind of person you are does not change. You are still fat, just a little less than before.

If you achieve the goal of becoming "more trim", what are you? Here, you may or may not already consider yourself to be trim but you are in the process of becoming trimmer. Becoming trimmer is much more enjoyable than being less fat. Also be aware, that I did not use the word skinny, but trim. The reason relates to health and how perception shapes our goals. I have never come across anyone who is too trim, but I have definitely met people that were too skinny.

Time to put it bluntly: **Always craft your statements and goals in a positive way. Focus on what you do want, not on what you don't want.**

There are two reasons for this. The first reason is that it feels better to focus on and expect to become ...

Trimmer, calmer and more confident as opposed to less stressed, anxious and fat! By focusing on what you do want you feel good about achieving your goals when you think about them. The second reason for a positive focus is that each individual word you use affects you.

When you use the words "less fat" or "not anxious," your brain still hears the words "fat" and "anxious." Even though you don't want to feel them, your brain must process and make you feel to some extent everything that is presented to it.

I will reveal why that is in the next chapter. Therefore it is always best to focus on what you do want and not on what you don't want. There is another benefit to this as well. Focusing on the positive often creates additional benefits to working on reducing the negative.

For example, most people who are struggling in their relationships have the wrong focus. They tell me they want to have fewer fights with their partner. Having less fights does not create a good relationship. What it will do is MAYBE lead to less conflict.

However, by wanting to have fewer fights, where is your attention. On fights! If you are thinking about fights, you feel the effects of previous fights and so there is a chance you could unknowingly be priming yourself for another fight right now, even though that is not what you want.

Assuming you do achieve the goal of "less fights", is your relationship now great? I have assisted many couples who "don't fight." They achieve this by rarely communicating. Not exactly a winning option. Many replace conflict with boredom, emotional distance or sadness. Hardly a victory.

However, what if the focus is on harmony? Not only will fewer fights naturally occur, because you can't be fighting when acting harmoniously, but the couple also grows in numerous ways because the focus is on creating something positive. The same goes for your individual health. Would you rather not be sick or be healthy? Not weak but strong? Less dumb or smarter?

You want to focus on winning, either jointly if in a team or individually, rather than on not losing. How often do you see it in sports and in other areas of life? Once someone stops trying to win and starts trying to not lose, they almost always lose. Whenever someone tries not to 'stuff up' rather than 'perform well,' they stuff it up big time.

Finally, let's go back to the racing car and the wall. Now consider what you should be thinking as you go into that corner. Something along the lines of "keep my line and stay focused on the road" I am sure. Always focus and craft your success statements and goals in a positive way. That way, you can train your brain to focus on the benefits and start to feel good whilst at the same time naturally reducing the likelihood of failure by simply continuing to keep your energy, focus and eyes on the prize.

Principle Summary

Positive Focus: Learn the simplest and most effective positive thinking habit.

Focus on what you do want and not on what you don't want. Seek out and actively practice using the most empowering words, images and ideas in relation to your goals.

Fast-Action Techniques

1. Write out what you do want to happen in relation to three upcoming goals or interactions. For example, "I am going to have a fun and connected dinner with my friend/colleague/mother etc. where I will be on time, and we will speak calmly and harmoniously."
2. Think about the actual words and phrases you regularly use and change them to make them more positively focused. Start with just one disempowering word or phrase a day if you like. Your goal is to be trim, fit and healthy, exciting and dynamic, interesting and vibrant. It should not be about becoming less fat, sloppy or sick, dull or reserved and so on.
3. Use positive imagery and practice expecting success even when things go wrong (e.g. staying calm or confident regardless of an issue arising) when considering upcoming tasks or events. Imagine yourself remaining correctly focused and behaving as positively as possible and working through any issues until a great final outcome is achieved and all key people are satisfied.

Hypnotic Recording – A Winning Mind through Positive Focus and Optimism: For guided assistance in moving beyond the principles and techniques of this chapter, a guided brain retraining process to assist you in developing the winner's mindset through optimism and positive focus is currently available at - http://mentalhealthhypnosis.com/positivefocusandoptimism

Mindful Acceptance
Overcome negative thinking through mindfulness training exercises for stress reduction and positive wellbeing

You cannot control your mind. You can inspire, trigger, lead and focus it, but STOP TRYING TO FULLY CONTROL IT! You will lose, every time!

I assume you are familiar with the metaphor of "the elephant in the room." It relates to the idea that there is something in the room (either a physical room or your mind), and the more you try to avoid it, the more obvious it becomes.

Imagine there actually was an elephant residing in your living room. You have no idea how it got there and you would very much like it to leave. You are afraid of its size and its power and you feel it doesn't belong there. You can't push it out because it's too big. You tell it to leave but it doesn't listen. You try shouting at it, asking politely, commanding it and nothing works. Strangely, the more you try to make it go away, the larger and more burdensome it seems to become.

That's because you're putting all your attention on it. When you put more of your mental attention on something, it feels bigger; it takes up more of your mental space. The question is: Are you putting positive, neutral or negative attention on it? In this scenario, you are putting frustrated attention onto it, and so you're frustration will only increase.

What's the solution?

Stop fighting against the elephant. Accept it and let it be there. Perhaps you need to make a few adjustments and then continue to use your living room as before.

Now what happens?

Does it go away? It might! But, then again, it might not! It might get bored and leave but then come back another time. Regardless of what it does, the elephant will appear smaller now as you stop trying to force it away.

What's its purpose?

Elephants are large, stable, protective creatures. Your elephant guards the door to your living room and has a say in what comes in. Elephants are also known as patient and wise. Your elephant has something to teach you, it carries a message. However to receive the message you must be kind and patient towards it. You cannot force an elephant. Once the message is received, the elephant may then go to return another time, or may stay and continue to guard your living room door. Either way, you now are at peace with your elephant. You might even be able to go for a ride on it one day.

Whatever You Push Pushes Back

Just like the elephant, you cannot push away your experience. The more you try to suppress (push down or push away) your experiences, the more attention you give them and the more they push back. Trying not to feel, think, or remember something once it has been triggered never works.

Right now, don't think about an elephant in a room. Don't think about its color, or shape or that it is now eating chocolate cake. Now try to not notice the sensations in your left hand, or your right foot. Now try and not notice what it smells like around you? Now try and pretend that you didn't fail at everything I just asked you to do and notice how you fail at that too!

Dealing with Negative Thoughts

The reason why you can't not experience something once it is presented to you is because your brain must process everything that is presented to it to see if it is dangerous. The need for protection will always override logic. You can't help it. In fact, there is a very strong correlation between people who try to push down or push away experiences and those who suffer depression, anxiety and other major life challenges.

That potential danger can be physical like watching out for snakes that like to bite, but it can also be psychological. A psychological threat may be a fear of failure, embarrassment, poor performance, or rejection, basically any unknown experience that is going to lead you into feeling an emotion you generally don't like.

Your brain is always trying to protect you from feeling more pain than necessary. But, your brain isn't always right. Have you ever had to make a speech, and your brain started coming up with all sorts of catastrophic thoughts and images?

Things like: "They will all laugh at me, I won't know what I'm doing, I am going to get rejected and feel humiliated." When you actually look at all the times you presented before, none of these things even came close to happening.

Unfortunately that won't stop your brain initially from trying to protect you from a possible danger. One option is to reframe negative thoughts (look at Optimism Wins) and to continually practice Positive Focus. However, these are not perfect systems; you will still have negative thoughts at times.

To deal with this we need to remember the very first principle: Behavior is King! A thought is just a thought until you believe it and act on it. If you accept the thought for what it is, "just a thought," your brain has a chance to process it without you trying to get rid of it.

Because you're allowing the thought or image or sensation to be there, your brain has a chance to process it to see if it is dangerous or not. Because it realizes it is not, the power of the thought will reduce, and the thought itself is also likely to be processed and pass more quickly.

Going back to public speaking, you now know that your brain has come up with all these catastrophic scenarios to try and protect you. Rather than trying to force them away, if you accept that it is just your brain trying to protect you and you know that they will pass in its own time, those fearful thoughts will pass much more quickly. At the same time, you continue to implement your positive focus principles.

Mindfulness as the Science and Art of Acceptance

Knowing that acceptance is the key, the question is how to make it a skill? It is easier said than done, especially when emotions are high. The art is learning how to become a better observer of your internal world, to look at the elephant without reacting negatively to it.

Mindfulness, which is a form of meditation, can easily be described as simple and highly calming exercises of attention, awareness and focus. Mindfulness has been shown to increase energy, focus, concentration, creativity, intelligence, memory, learning ability, inner calm, happiness, self-esteem, overall health, and reduce stress, anxiety and depression.

It is the most successfully researched mental health building and mental illness reducing skill. Consistent practice changes lives and re-wires brains. Mindfulness exercises have been shown to be an incredibly powerful way to shift down into the longer brain wave states that give you access to your intuition, numerous unconscious processes and all of the abilities mentioned above.

Meditation and hypnosis allow you to go deep into your unconscious mind and begin building new pathways in your brain which will translate to a greater ability to learn, problem solve and stay calm when facing difficult situations.

Mindfulness trains your focus and attention. It allows you to take a break from the "chatter" and busyness of your active mind. It is a fantastic way to find a neutral (usually slightly positive) feeling and be able to enjoy the moment you are in now and develop a greater appreciation of all that is around you.

So, how does it work? Informally, all you need to do is choose a sense and immerse yourself into it. You can pretty much do it anywhere, anytime. Due to mindfulness, I am pretty much never bored! Whenever I am stuck somewhere waiting for something, I practice different mindfulness exercises.

As I said, all you need to do is choose a sense and immerse yourself in it.

(**Important Bonus**: Because mindfulness, like hypnosis is much easier to follow by listening than reading (especially hypnosis), I have decided to give you three mindfulness recordings to listen to with this book. You can get all three of them at the following link - http://mentalhealthhypnosis.com/freemindfulnessdownloads)

However, you can still develop some of your mindfulness skills now. Let's begin...

We'll begin with vision. Sit up nice and tall and begin to breathe more deeply if you like. Now expand your vision and notice everything that is around you. Spend some time noticing all the different colors, shapes and textures around you. Zone in on particular things and really look at them, examine them and enjoy noticing them.

Let's move on to a different sense, hearing!

Move your attention to what you can hear. Pick one constant sound and really zone in on it. Notice its rhythm, timbre and volume. Really immerse yourself in that sound. Then choose another sound and do the same.

Let's do one more sense for the time being, touch!

Wherever you are sitting, take the time now to zone in and really focus on where and how you are sitting. Notice the sensations of your feet against the floor...

Notice the sensations of your back and legs against the chair...

Notice your internal sensations now, perhaps the sensations in your hands or beating of your heart... and when you're ready, we can move on. Take your time and enjoy!

It's time you learnt a more formal exercise. This one will teach you to be able to move into that positively-neutral and self-observant place. In this exercise it is recommended that you close your eyes. So, you may want to read over this bit several times

Mindful Acceptance

before you do this. Or, you can download the recording now and listen to it which would make it much easier.

TAKE YOUR TIME WHEN YOU DO IT. ENJOY DOING IT SLOWLY!

The first part of this exercise requires you to create a visualization. I will give you three to choose from or you can make up one of your own: a conveyer belt, steam clouds evaporating, or a river with leaves on it. In the recording, the river is used.

During this exercise, every time you have a thought about anything at all, you are going to imagine taking that thought and either placing it on a conveyer belt to watch it be taken away, put it in an evaporating cloud, or put it onto a leaf in a river and let it float away. Only choose one image.

Whenever you have a thought, any thought, you are going to allow that thought to drift away. So choose a particular image and we will begin.

Close your eyes and firstly notice your breathing... notice as you breathe in and breathe out... pay attention to the sensations you feel, the rise and fall of your chest...

And, whatever thoughts you have, just let them go as you notice them.

Shift your attention to what you can hear. Like before chose one sound and just notice it for a while, then choose another, and perhaps a third.

Whatever thoughts you have, just let them go as you notice them each time they come.

Shift your attention to your body. Notice several different sensations one by one, starting with external and moving into internal, and whatever thoughts you have, just let them go each and every time.

Then bring your attention back to your breathing... and when you're ready you can open your eyes and stop.

There you go! A fantastic simple exercise you can practice daily to sharpen your awareness, focus, and concentration. Deepen your levels of calm by learning how to observe yourself and let go of thoughts and sensations. Mindfulness is something we will be returning to regularly as we proceed into the other sections of this book.

Principle Summary

Mindful Acceptance: Overcome negative thinking through mindfulness training exercises for stress reduction and positive wellbeing.

The more you try and suppress an internal experience, the more it will bounce back because your (often overprotective) brain must process it to check for danger and decide what to do about it. Acceptance of the (negative) experience, whilst still focusing and acting on what you do want, allows for faster processing (greater habituation – to be explained in "Expose Yourself" chapter) and more meaningful living to occur.

Fast-Action Techniques

1. Daily mindfulness practice is highly recommended. Use the above script or the recordings to practice one formal exercise, 5-10 minutes only a day. Just 5 minutes a day of silence is great for your mental health. It is usually good to practice before any stressful events or before bed, especially if you struggle to let go of your worries at the end of the day.
2. After any mindfulness practice, reflect on the experience and seek any lessons that may have arisen from your experience. It is often good to mindfully contemplate a problem after you have done your practice as your mind will be calmer and open to finding more unique solutions.
3. Challenge yourself to practice when out and about, even if it is in very short increments. You can do anything mindfully, by choosing one sense at a time and fully focussing on it. You

can wash dishes mindfully or observe all the drivers around you when stuck in traffic, during a conversation or when waiting in a queue and so on.

Part 2: The Principles of Enhancing Mood and Living Well

Pure Pleasures
Uncover the foundation of happiness and key activities to move away from depression

Why does someone hate their life?

Answer: Because they spend most of their days doing things they don't enjoy.

Life is difficult and we all have responsibilities that are dull, difficult, and sometimes, just plain depressing. These need to be balanced out with activities you enjoy. This is especially essential for those currently in unfulfilling careers or other lifestyle situations.

Sometimes just asking the simple question "how can I make this activity more enjoyable?" will lead to a beneficial insight, like listening to your favorite music or watching interesting videos or having foam fights to improve the experience of washing dishes.

The foundation of happiness is pleasure. Pleasure can be defined as any positive emotion that you feel which is caused by any activity that you enjoy. The seeking of pleasure underlines everything that we do. Even when we decide to do an activity that we know will not be pleasurable in the short term (like those dishes or that job), we do it in the hope of it leading to an eventual outcome that will be pleasurable.

A life of pleasure is of course not the only thing required for great mental health and a satisfying life, but a life with little to no pleasure will lead to burn-out. Sadly, feeling less pleasure is one of the first symptoms of depression. Therefore, it is critical that pleasure be a respected part of your life.

One secret to happiness and good mental health is to understand what your favorite and most pleasurable activities are and know how to use them in order to increase the quality of your life. I have broken up the pleasurable things that make people happy into two categories. The categories are **Regular Pleasures** and **Reward Pleasures.**

In daily life, it is important to have a few standard pleasures that are practiced regularly to make life enjoyable, but in order to pull yourself towards growing as a person and achieving your greater goals, you need to create reward pleasures that you can only receive once you have earned them. One of the deep problems of modern life is that many people are so used to getting what they want when they want it, that they will never experience the full pleasure that comes from a reward that they have worked to earn.

Up until 2008, there was a 40 year period where every year the rate of overall wealth in Western countries grew exponentially. Even with all the extra material wealth, compared to all previous generations, luxury item debts continued to climb ludicrously high. Even with all that extra wealth and all the extra luxury items, people overall had not become any happier and on the flipside, over that same time period depression increased tenfold.

Why?

That is because the novelty of a fancy toy or experience that you did not work hard to obtain wears off quite quickly. You cannot live a non-challenging lifestyle and expect to feel intense pleasure. However, if your toy or experience is an honest and fair reward based on what you have accomplished, then the potential pleasure that comes from that reward once you receive it is much greater.

Have you ever worked really hard on a goal and found that when you finally finished it and gave yourself a reward, it felt so much better than it would normally? It can even be something simple. If you have been working hard on a project and your goal is to have it finished before dinner, doesn't dinner often taste better when you know you have finished your goal? What happens when you give yourself a reward before you've earned it? Well, it can still feel good temporarily but it doesn't last anywhere near as long and you may start to feel anxious, stressed and guilty.

When you do reward yourself after finishing a goal, you tend to feel the pleasurable emotions of relaxation, excitement and freedom. Sometimes, you do need to just give yourself a short break, even if you haven't finished your task, especially if you have started to fatigue and are becoming ineffective. In this case, you want to set achievable mini-goals that you can reach before taking any short breaks, and have a simple plan made for what to do once you return to the task.

Knowing that pleasure is the foundation of happiness, let's look at how you can increase the total amount of pleasure in your life.

Finding Pleasure Exercise

Write out a list of your current regular pleasures (e.g. television shows, social engagements, sports, reading, hobbies, creative pursuits, etc.) in your life and your larger pleasures (e.g. new products, holidays, special events, etc.).

Then rank your regular pleasures in order of importance and plan how you could increase the time you spend on your favorites and decrease the time spent on ones that are not that enjoyable.

Set aside specific time each week to sing, dance, play games and spend time with positive friends. **DO NOT participate in these activities in a half-baked way**. Fully focus and engage in them. Remove all possible distractions while you do them. With your larger reward pleasures, write down what important activities you need to accomplish first (and within what time frame, review goal setting chapter for more on this) before rewarding yourself with them.

Emergency Specific Pleasure Prompts

As a general rule, the regular and reward pleasures system is a great method to keep life enjoyable.

Unfortunately, sometimes people can fall into depressive and de-motivated moods where a goal focused pleasures system will be too difficult. The secret in this scenario is to create a list of pleasure prompts. However, this can be hard for someone to do alone when they are feeling depressed. With patience and by asking the right questions, I can get even the most stuck person to create a list of at least a dozen things. Of course, having a trained professional to assist is a luxury most people don't have when needed most.

There is a better option which is to act now! You should create your pleasure prompts list when you are feeling fine and continue to add to it whenever a new idea comes up. Ask friends and colleagues what they enjoy and if you enjoy them too, add it to the list. One of the advantages of modern technology is not only can we put our list on our phone so it will be with us wherever we go, we can also easily and quickly access video, audio and text when we need it.

Pleasure Prompts List and Set-up

Right now, create a favorites list. Don't think, just write. All you need is at least five in total. Write down 1-3 of your favorites in each of the following categories: songs, jokes, books (book passages), poems, videos/movies, sports, hobbies, sensory joys (bath, massage, intimacy, cooking), friends, games, dances. Keep this list in your wallet or electronically on your phone and make these options easily accessible.

Put your favorite songs, images or videos on your phone (or links for where they can be easily streamed), your favorite jokes, poems and books (or at least book passages) on your desk and in your phone. Have maps and apps for key places of interest. Keep special folders with cherished photographs and social activities to do alone or with friend's.

As a general rule, avoid computer games and alcohol as they can be addictive and depressive in the medium to long term. Stick with prompts that normally inspire or rejuvenate you. Even if you are not feeling inspired at the time, the principles of "acting now" and "movement" will lead to greater pleasurable momentum. The key is not to overthink it. If struggling, immediately scan your list and do the first thing you find that you can start without delay. That is why your list should always be with you and ready. When in doubt - open, scan, pick whatever seems easiest and begin!

The more you engage with the activity, the more effective it will be. If you're going to listen to your favorite song, listen deeply or better yet, sing along as passionately as you can. Dance freely, read that poem out loud, make that bath just right, turn off the TV and your computer and put your phone on airplane mode and really talk, walk or play games with your friends, colleagues or kids if suitable and so on.

Principle Summary

Pure Pleasures: Uncover the foundation of happiness and key activities to move away from depression.

Pleasurable activities are the fastest and simplest way to build positive mood. You should have easy on-hand access to a list of favorites (with key ones being immediately available) to use when in need of a positive emotional boost. If mood is ever very low, select whatever you will enjoy most and is easiest for you to do and begin it immediately.

Fast-Action Techniques

1. If you have not already, right now create your pleasure prompts list and schedule your weekly planning time for your regular and reward pleasures.
2. Explore at least three activities you regularly do that are not pleasurable and consider what you could add or change to the experience to make it more pleasurable. For example, if related to a chore, could you add music, do it with a friend, change the lighting, or sing or dance while you do it. Or, of course, do it mindfully.
3. Take a big picture look at your career and home life and look for gaps where you may feel bored or unfulfilled. Consider what you should change (big or small) to make life more enjoyable overall and write out a plan of action in order to implement the change. Review goal setting chapter to assist if needed.

Hypnotic Recording – The Pure Pleasures Experience: For guided assistance in moving beyond the principles and techniques of this chapter, a guided brain re-training process to assist you in enjoying the pleasures of life in a much deeper way where you have greater joy, fun and aliveness and increase chances of more bliss and ecstasy type experiences is available now at this link - http://mentalhealthhypnosis.com/pleasure

A Real and Supportive Social Life
How to find new friends, increase chances of romance and reduce social anxiety and shyness

Why do people who live in large cities, often surrounded by people, often feel more alone than those living in smaller towns?

How can people with thousands of fans, "friends," and followers on social media say they feel lonely?

Have you ever felt a friendly urge to talk to someone you didn't know and then backed away at the last moment?

Unless you are autistic, you are a social creature. Connecting to other humans is important to you. It is vital for your mental health. The history of societal progress is built on groups. Family and community groups orchestrated the destiny of human life. Your brain is also built to enjoy the company of others. In it are mirror neurons, and they are designed to help you understand the expressions of others and amplify the feelings you receive during positive social experiences.

Good social support is the number one protective factor against mental illness. It is also often the most important factor during a difficult time. Often the first question asked when someone is in emotional turmoil is not "what" but "who can you go to for help?"

Sometimes a smile from a stranger, the simplest act of kindness, will save a person's life. I've heard this story more than once, where for whatever reason the receipt of a smile inspired the person enough to avoid taking their life and seeking help.

Ironically, it seems that the "whats," and the "things" in our life receive much more attention than the people. This creates a world of "artificial engagement," which is one of the seven mental viruses I see plaguing modern society. How much can you connect with someone with headphones in their ears, eyes on a screen and fingers constantly swiping and tapping on a piece of glass?

You are not really speaking to all of them, but just a part of their shell, their social avatar. The art of full communication is dying. This is creating reduced self-esteem, social awkwardness and a lack of understanding between people. Humans are designed to communicate and taking too many short cuts and not having enough 1-on-1, distraction-less, in-person engagement is creating real problems. Not only can technology be distracting, it also allows people to hide truer aspects of themselves that are essential for the deepest relationships.

When we meet someone new, or even when we talk to someone we know about something important, some anxiety is likely to be felt. Although it is rare that we perceive a physical threat, we are always on the lookout for psychological and social threats. Because we are living in a heavily consumer focused society, artificial engagement can also be a useful protective mechanism.

With so much advertising and the knowledge that some unethical people will try to take advantage of you, shutting out information becomes important. You do need to learn how to listen to your instincts around some people and be selective with whom you engage. However it is not wise to avoid everyone just so we can protect ourselves.

Since we are designed to seek the company of others, we tend to be very careful about how we present ourselves and the impression we make. If we feel we may not be able to make a good impression, the urge will be to avoid social interaction and communicate through less confronting means like chat and email, or not at all. A greater emotional and social irresponsibility also occurs as people nowadays end relationships through text, email, and even social media posts. An over-reliance on these artificial channels kills social and emotional skills.

All major life skills are learnt. The ability to read body language, tonality and emotions has declined in many people. Without these fundamental skills, the ability to understand someone at the deepest level becomes impossible and relationships that have the potential to become engaging and enriching remain shallow, functional and lifeless. This is how you can be surrounded by people both online and offline and still feel alone.

The Online Fantasy

Almost everything you experience online is built on a foundation of fantasy. Pictures are photo-shopped, videos are manipulated, social media updates are highly skewed towards the overblown. The more time you spend online, the greater the risk that you will start to feel inadequate as you compare yourself to the fantasy.

A good deal of research is demonstrating how too much time online is making people feel depressed. People see how others appear to be having a much better life than they and wonder why their life as great isn't. All the advertising doesn't help either. **THAT'S BECAUSE IT'S NOT REAL!**

How can you compete with a fantasy? In order to compete, some people become highly self-obsessed and narcissistic as they try to improve their online image. A much better solution is to restrict your time online, especially on social media and instead seek deeper and truer relationships.

How to Find Real Friends

The reality is most of us develop friendships through proximity. When we were younger, most of our friends were from school. When older, we found friends usually from work. However, those avenues can dry up.

Many people I have worked with who were seeking new friendships are totally confused about how to make new friends. The common response is "I don't like pubs and clubs." My response is pubs and clubs are full of alcohol, noise and self-contained groups of people generally making them horrible places to try to meet people and get to know them.

My recommendation is always interest groups. Consider what you are interested in and join a group or do courses related to that: sports, arts, crafts, community, outdoors, even support groups that help people overcome certain problems or just plain and simple social gathering groups.

There are hundreds of them, and if you don't know where to start, begin with the website "Meetup." Type the word into your search engine, go to the site, search for the one in your country, type in where you live and dozens of options will start to pop up. The best thing about being part of an interest group is there is much less pressure to be something you are not or find a topic to talk about. You are all naturally interested in the same topic, so talk about that! This should help reduce any potential social anxiety or shyness (for specific social confidence techniques see the Social Skills chapter). The more groups you join, the more people you meet and the greater the chance of developing deeper friendships.

Finding a Partner

People in relationships have been shown time and time again to be happier than those who are not. Most of us seek to be in a relationship. Once again, proximity is how most people find their partner, as adults that usually means through work. However, this is not always appropriate.

Many people these days use online dating sites and almost every person, I've ever seen professionally who has used them, has disliked the experience. The reason why is simply because the online fantasy rarely matches the in-person reality.

Once again I think joining social interest groups is the key. That way you get to meet people who actually share at least one similar interest with you, the environment is relaxed and non-threatening and you have a chance to really get to know someone before exploring whether a date is possible. If there is no one suitable in that particular group, you can always join an additional group and still have a good time pursuing your interests.

Keeping Friends and Partners

At the last minute, I decided to add a bonus chapter on this topic. If you can't wait to read it, I'll summarize the three key points. The first is when in doubt, aim to meet up and connect over your main shared interest. Secondly, utilize positive focus principles when communicating. The key questions to ask yourself will be things like "how can we have more harmony and more fun" as opposed to less fights or less boredom. Third is use praise as often as possible. It is the ultimate social tool. Emotions are contagious and positive expressions will create an amplifying loop of goodwill, build trust and deepen your relationships. All these skills and additional ones as well will be more deeply addressed in the Praise Pays and two Bonus Chapters.

If you Need Help - Get it!

The reality is sometimes friends and family are simply not emotionally equipped to deal with certain problems. Do your research and see a highly recommended professional who will be right there with you, one on one. If unsure, seek advice from your family doctor. As a psychologist, I sometimes forget how powerful and healing I can be before I even open my mouth. For some people, just knowing they are going to receive my full, undivided, uninterrupted and non-judgmental attention for close to an hour is very healing in and of itself.

Principle Summary

A Real and Supportive Social Life: How to find new friends, increase chances of romance and reduce social anxiety and shyness.

Humans are social creatures and positive social environments stimulate creativity, self-expression and personal growth. The easiest way to meet, learn to be inspired and feel supported by like-minded people (and build friendships or romances) is to join interest groups.

Fast-Action Techniques

1. Do an online search (e.g. Meetup) or speak to current social contacts in order to research a new interest group. Once you find 1-3, immediately make contact with the groups, even if you have no plans of joining them in the near future. Just saying hello and that you have an interest in that area should be enough to start a conversation and better explore if it could be a good fit for you.

2. If very shy and seeking to make a good first impression, keep it simple. Put yourself in a confident physiology (review movement chapter if needed), head up, shoulders back, breathing deep etc. and simply say "hello" with a strong and welcoming voice and aiming to make eye contact. Start by saying "hello" and keep moving along with at least three people a day. This should be done even if you are very shy, as making regular and truly engaging social contact as opposed to artificially engaging others is still important for our mental health. When done correctly, this tends to create a positive emotional boost. If seeking a full conversation process, review the social skills chapter.
3. A large part of the process for finding the right people to connect to is trusting your intuition based on first impressions. These are called 'snap judgements' and they tend to be quite accurate when properly followed. Below is a process to help you learn how to review and better create your own first impressions.

Snap Judgements Review and Creation Process

Key: Ensure you answer every question and sub-question set out in the following process, using a previously important interaction and/or event as the source.

1. **Review Emotions** – Tune in to how you felt during the event. What were you feeling when with him or her? Did you feel more positive emotions like excited, energetic, comfortable, joyful; or more negative emotions like uncertain, bored, edgy, or disappointed?
2. **Review Physicality** – How frequent was eye contact? How close did you sit or stand to each other, and how did it feel? Did one of you pull back or edge forward as it progressed? Was body language open or closed, and was there any physical contact? How did the conversation feel and sound? Did it seem respectful, fun, and flowing or was it stilted and awkward?

A Real and Supportive Social Life

3. **Quality of Contact** – What was the quality of the physical contact (handshake or hand on shoulder), if any? Whether you touched each other or not, did it feel right as an idea? Did they look you in the eyes when shaking your hand or away? Did they smile or did it seem more obligatory? Were they simply going through the motions, or did it feel genuine? Did the contact, if made, feel right in regard to firmness?
4. *OPTIONAL: What could you have done differently to have enhanced the interaction? Could you have smiled more, spoken with more authority or less, listened more, engaged in more eye contact, changed your body language, touched more or less, and so on? From all these considerations, choose three in particular and consciously aim to use them in your next important set of interactions.

Hypnotic Recording – Superior Social Skills: For guided assistance in moving beyond the principles and techniques of this chapter, a guided brain re-training process to assist you in making a great first impression, increasing social attractiveness and confidence and positively connecting to others with greater ease is at this link - http://mentalhealthhypnosis.com/superiorsocialskills

Optimism Wins
Increase emotional intelligence with Positive Psychology's biggest secret to life success

You are about to watch a race: the Olympic 100 metre final. You see eight muscular, chiselled human beings all at the top of their game. It is almost time. All those years of training, dreaming and sacrifice. Every member of the crowd has the same question on their mind. "Who will win?" Will it be the favorite, or is a surprise victory on the cards?

As you look at the athletes' faces, you wonder, "what are they thinking?" This is actually pretty easy to answer. If they are all mentally prepared, then they will all be thinking the same thing. **"I'm going to win!"** This doesn't seem to make sense. There can only be one winner. Or, can there? Officially, that is correct, only one person will be crowned champion, but unofficially they could all win.

If every athlete is mentally prepared and willing to do their very best, then every athlete grows and develops and becomes more than they were before. Even if they lose, they win. It is this mentality, the persistent expectation of winning that allowed them to get this far in their career in the first place. Without it, they would have given up years ago and never reached the level of skill they now have.

Of course there are other factors contributing to their success as well: talent, skill, training, genes, nutrition and so on. However, a winning mindset is the crown of all skill development. If you have the right mentality, even when you lose, your winning expectation if backed by proper preparation and effort will force you to improve, and so you win. You will not always obtain the official winner's title, but the prize of personal growth and self-respect is always available.

Most of us have heard the classic question, is the glass "half empty" or "half full?" This question is reflective of the perceptual difference between a pessimist and an optimist. As a cheeky optimist, I like to move beyond the question and say, "it's half full but

I don't care because I will drink straight from the bottle and I know how to get into the factory." A severe pessimist would probably say, "It's half empty and probably poisoned." Sadly poison is quite an appropriate word, as pessimism is likely to poison your attitude and potential.

The question is do you need to be an optimist to be successful, mentally healthy and happy? The answer is it depends on the context. There are always exceptions to the rule, but as an overall style of thinking, optimism is much healthier. In fact, optimistic self-talk (refers to how you think, imagine and speak about yourself) has been found to be the biggest predictor of life success

Pessimism carries the opposite attitude and beliefs as optimism. Pessimism is a style of thinking and belief found in the depressed. So what is optimism? Optimism is not blind positive thinking and belief. Rather it is an <u>empowering</u> style of thinking used to explain the cause of an event. How you interpret the <u>cause of events</u> will shape your future beliefs and decisions. *Often the term used for how you interpret an event is a frame. To change your thinking about a situation is to reframe it.*

There are three main factors that will determine your level of optimism.

The first factor is **Permanence**.

<u>Pessimists</u> believe that the <u>bad things</u> that happen in their life are **permanent**.

<u>Optimists</u> believe that the <u>bad things</u> that happen in their life are **temporary**.

Pessimists tend to give up more easily than optimists because they feel helpless. What is the point of trying if you believe bad things will just continue to happen anyway? Over time the pessimist through lack of trying will train themselves to be helpless. This is how learned helplessness develops which is where people give up on problems very quickly, well before they should.

To illustrate the key mindset differences between the two and the results that can occur, one study asked a group of pessimists and optimists to estimate how well they would do on a test. What they found was that the pessimists were initially more accurate and the optimists tended to over-estimate how well they would do.

You would think this to be a victory for the pessimists, right? Yes and no. Although the pessimists were more accurate initially, with each additional test, the optimists worked harder to achieve what they believed they were capable of and over-time continued to improve their performance whilst the pessimists stagnated.

Once again, even when you lose, if you keep improving, you win!

Pessimists use words like "always" and "never." Optimists use words like "sometimes," "recently," "currently," and "occasionally" to explain bad events.

PERMANENT (PESSIMIST): Thinks - "I'll never figure this out," "You always forget the list," "My neighbour hates me," "You always insult me".

TEMPORARY (OPTIMIST): Thinks - "I'll solve this once I am settled," "You sometimes forget it when we are in a rush," "My neighbour looks unusually angry today," and "You insult me when you're tired and stressed".

When referring to good events, the opposite effect occurs.

TEMPORARY (PESSIMIST): Thinks - "They got bored and let me win," "I got lucky," "I did well due to having done it before."

PERMANENT (OPTIMIST): Thinks - "I won because I worked harder," "I am lucky," "I always create great results."

The second factor is **Pervasive**.

Pervasive is the next component and refers to whether you see the causes of events as "specific" to the situation or more "universal or global" across numerous life situations.

People who give universal explanations for their failures tend to give up on a number of things even when they only failed in one particular area. Someone who gives a specific explanation realizes that they may have failed in that area, but believe there are many other areas of life where they will be successful.

UNIVERSAL (PESSIMIST): Thinks - "I always fail," "No one likes me," "All managers are useless."

SPECIFIC (OPTIMIST): Thinks - "I failed that particular task," "That person does not like me," "2 of the 5 managers are not performing to requirements."

In regards to positive events, the optimist believes that good events are expected and are due to the skills and abilities they already have. The pessimist believes a success is due to a narrower, more specific cause.

SPECIFIC (PESSIMIST): Thinks - "I knew a couple of good jokes," "My trainer only understands cardio training," "I impressed that client."

UNIVERSAL (OPTIMIST): Thinks - "I am funny," "My trainer is a total health and fitness expert," "I am impressive to all of my clients."

Optimists tend to create hope, while pessimists tend to create hopelessness. Having the ability to find permanent and universal causes for prosperous events and temporary and specific causes for adversity is the skill of the optimist and the foundation of hope.

How we see our future will influence our current mood. Optimists, despite adversity, are always hopeful of future improvements in life (to EXPECT success is even better). Pessimists, despite success, still feel hopeless and develop a hardship based vision of their future.

The final factor is **Personalization** and this relates to whether causes of events are believed to be due to internal or external factors. Optimists generally believe external events are responsible for when things go wrong.

For example, the optimist will generally state that it was the actions of other people that caused a particular problem. Optimists tend to have increased confidence and feel less guilt and shame unlike Pessimists who tend to blame themselves for almost everything.

On the plus side, this allows the optimist to have higher self-esteem than a pessimist, but optimists may also deny responsibility when they are the cause of a problem. This is why we need to keep the critical voice in our head employed, but in a position where he or she has a voice but does not make the major decisions.

All people, including optimists, need to monitor their actions accurately and accept responsibility for their mistakes.

The difference is, the optimist, if he or she is intelligent and open to learning, will see the mistake as a specific and temporary lapse and will use optimistic self-talk and find a way to improve. The pessimist will generalize the situation and see it as a permanent character flaw and use pessimistic self-talk to further exacerbate the problem and more than likely give up. At the end of the day, it is not about who is more right or wrong as reality is subjective anyway. It is about accessing potential and an optimist is more likely to strive to reach their full potential and experience greater enjoyment of the learning process as well.

The following table is a summary of the differences to keep in mind.

	PESSIMISTS	**OPTIMISTS**
Permanence		
Positive events	Temporary causes	Permanent causes
Negative events	Permanent causes	Temporary causes
Pervasiveness		
Positive events	Specific reasons	Global reasons
Negative events	Global reasons	Specific reasons
Personalization		
Positive events	External causes	Internal causes
Negative events	Internal causes	External causes

Principle Summary

Optimism Wins: Increase emotional intelligence with Positive Psychology's biggest secret to life success.

Being an optimist and expecting success will give you more positive control in your life. You will create self-fulfilling prophecies and naturally improve in ways you won't even realize.

Fast-Action Techniques

1. Think of an optimist you know and a pessimist. Describe what you like and dislike about each person's personality and the benefits and limitations of each. Then write out how they would handle a difficult situation. Consider both points of view and what you can learn from each one.
2. Write out your usual self-talk in three challenging situations. Examples may be how you would think during a job review, a date, joining a new class and so on. Use the previous reframing examples and tables as a guide in order to optimistically re-write your self-talk.
3. For one week, whenever you notice yourself being pessimistic, or feel stuck, ask yourself: "how would an optimist view and respond to this situation?" You can ask the question as is, and/or you could also consider it from the perspective of an optimistic role-model's perspective.

Hypnotic Recording – A Winning Mind through Positive Focus and Optimism: For guided assistance in moving beyond the principles and techniques of this chapter, a guided brain re-training process to assist you in developing the winner's mindset through optimism and positive focus is available now at this link - http://mentalhealthhypnosis.com/positivefocusandoptimism

New-You Nutrition
Lose weight, stop emotional eating and avoid the latest diets and weight loss scams by uncovering how to eat without obsession

It's now time to reveal the ultimate diet. This is it! The one you've been waiting for. The secret and "super easy" solution where you can "eat what you want" and still have instant energy, better skin, higher strength and greater weight loss. It's called the "Be a Sucker Diet." However, that is its secret name. It actually changes its name constantly, because the "Be a Sucker Diet" is really whatever diet is "hot" right now. This is how the "diet" industry continues to suck billions of dollars from people's bank accounts every year.

What you consume is, of course, extremely important for your mental health. We are physical and biological creatures, and so the better the energy sources, the better we operate. Unfortunately, the majority of people I see with depression and anxiety issues admit to having poor nutritional habits, usually worsening since starting to feel depressed and anxious. It becomes a perpetual bad habit cycle where poor nutrition leads to feeling worse and feeling worse continues to stimulate poorer nutrition.

A diet is not the answer! Massive and sudden nutritional modifications and/or restrictions to instigate large weight reductions are rarely maintained, activate a biological starvation reflex and almost always lead to more than the original weight lost being put back on. In addition, increased risk of health problems occur with each "yo-yo" diet cycle.

There are thousands of nutritional books out there with some based on solid scientific research and most being rubbish. It is of course beyond the scope of this book to go into nutrition in great detail. This is a book of principles. *You will need to do your own research and keep your medical history and food beliefs in mind in order to specify what is best for you.* However, I am extremely confident you could make some very significant and sustainable changes by following the principles and guidelines I'll set out.

In my opinion, uncovering principles for optimal nutrition is actually pretty easy to do. The question I've always asked is "what are the core foods consumed by a professional athlete leading up to competition?" Most athletes consume (and don't consume) the same core foods and fluids. The amounts will be different between sports, but the types of foods and fluids consumed (and not consumed) are often the same.

Athletic Eating Guidelines

- **Rule of thumb:** Whole and fresh food is championed. Pre-made and pre-packaged items are avoided.
- **Major Protein:** Use "lean" protein sources. This includes grilled, steamed or baked (generally not fried) skinless chicken, game, and other lean meat. Also good are most types of fish. The following is also fine for vegetarians: tofu, beans and legumes, egg whites (generally no more than two yolks per day as they contain higher fat and cholesterol) and correctly used protein powders (whey being most common).
- **Complex Carbohydrates:** Focus on wholegrain breads and cereals like oatmeal, brown rice and whole wheat pasta, 1-2 baked potatoes a day (traditional or sweet), beans, and barley.
- **Dairy:** Include fat free or low fat (and sugar) milk, yoghurt and cheese.
- **Vegetables and fruit:** All green vegetables are eaten without restriction and an addition to most meals. Other vegetables in moderation are also fine. Fruit (due to high sugar) usually should be limited to 1-2 pieces a day.
- **Antioxidants:** Include a handful of berries. Blueberries and raspberries tend to be best.
- **Raw Nuts:** Include a handful of raw nuts. Any is fine, almonds tend to be best.
- **Cooking Oils:** Olive Oil tends to be healthiest (cold pressed extra virgin being the highest quality). Vegetable, canola and most other oils and butter are avoided.

- **Correct fats:** Most of the good fats you need will be in the range of foods above. Fish is especially good for polyunsaturated fat and nuts, avocado (half a day) and olives (in your oil too) for monounsaturated. Saturated and trans-fats will be mostly avoided as they feature heavily in pre-packaged food.
- **Supplements:** Use multivitamin, fish oil, glucosamine, flaxseed, and others depending on doctor recommendations.
- **Drink:** Drink unlimited water. You may also have 1-2 cups of sugar free coffee or tea, and 1-2 cups of skim/low fat milk total. 1-2 fresh vegetable juices, 1 vegetable juice with a piece of fruit is usually fine or 1 small cup of fresh juice is fine. Larger cups of high sugar fruit juice should be avoided. Juice drinks, cordial, soft drinks, energy drinks and alcohol should be strictly avoided. Sports drinks are only ever used in a sporting context.
- **Avoid:** Avoid pre-made and pre-packaged foods, especially anything with more than 10g per 100g of refined sugar, less than 3g per 100g saturated fat, less than 120mg per 100g of sodium (salt), white rice and white flour.

Classic athletic eating guidelines

Every athlete is of course different and so is every nutritional plan. Some athletes avoid dairy, some are even more restrictive in terms of complex carbohydrates, fruits and so on. What I can say is if the average person adhered to these guidelines (factoring in any dietary or medical issues) the results in terms of overall health, correct weight maintenance and energy would be extremely impressive. These are the food guidelines I follow most of the time.

The classic rule of thumb in the athletic world in terms of proportions is 55-60% lean protein, 40-45% carbohydrate and 5-10% fats and sugars.

The formula for changing your weight is both very simple and yet challenging at the same time. It is calories consumed vs calories burnt by the body. It is challenging because burning is based on how much you move and the speed of your metabolism. Everyone's metabolism is different so trial and error is the only way to move towards greater measurement precision over time. However, for most people, precise measurement of calories consumed and how often you move (which of course includes exercise) is not necessary.

Getting "Real" and "Practical"

Over 50% of people in numerous Western countries are overweight. In simple terms, they eat far too much (especially far too much pre-packaged high in unsaturated/trans-fat and sugar food and drink) and move way too little (often without any regular scheduled exercise). I know most people would look at the guidelines I provide and say "I'm not going to just eat that?" That was never my expectation for most people, at least not straight away. I simply thought it was important to actually outline what healthy eating looks like.

The key for most people is not to suddenly demand a massive change in eating habits as we run the risk of moving towards a diet mentality. Rather, it is about making simple nutritional *additions, replacements and eliminations* (ARE). This is who you ARE to become. You choose one from each category and only work those three areas until you feel you have adjusted to the change (could be up to a few weeks) before moving on to the next cycle.

For example, you could add a handful of nuts or berries or more lean meat or fish, replace white rice or pasta with brown rice or brown pasta, and *eliminate* (or severely restrict if eliminating appears too difficult at first or is not the desired goal) soft drinks, alcohol, cakes, biscuits, chocolate, chips and so on. You only need to choose one of each, complete an adjustment cycle and once done, you ARE ready for another round.

If I was to suggest three to start with that would lead to the absolute best weight reduction results for the average person, it would be: Add much more water, replace sugary breakfast cereals with wholegrain oatmeal and eliminate soft drinks. Also, people think they can save time and still eat healthily with "fat free" frozen dinners. Unfortunately most are not good to have more than occasionally as even though there are ones who also have low sugar, they tend to be very high in sodium (salt). Always check the nutritional information.

Environmental and Eating Principles

Your environment plays a massive part in food. Create a strict shopping list, plan your meals and do not shop when you're hungry. Proximity is always an issue in relation to temptation and emotional eating. It is much easier to not eat chocolate when it is at the shop as opposed to in your cupboard. Remove the foods you don't want from the home and work environments.

If you know you should be eating less, start by taking 20% off your usual plate during meal times and have a glass of water before starting. Aim to eat mindfully and accept whatever cravings or emotions you feel. Before each mouthful, first imagine having a slow bite and focus on the taste to be enjoyed from that one bite. Then proceed to eat that one bite as you imagined it and continue with the process until the meal is complete. You will feel full faster and require less food by focusing on the quality and taste of each bite. Your third free mindfulness recording also outlines how you can enjoy eating mindfully.

Creating a Lifestyle with a Reduced Focus on Food

I rarely think about food and do not eat at all during 2/3 of my day. For 16 hours out of every 24-hour period, I drink only water and maybe one straight tea. It is called intermittent fasting. Humans have been fasting for thousands of years, sometimes due to lack of food but also often due to choice, and it is very much part of our biological history.

Evidence is still gathering for the benefits of intermittent fasting, but results look very promising. Not only does the practice suggest better digestion and rest for the organs, it is often associated with improved energy and weight reduction.

How it works: The idea is to shift what you normally eat into an 8-10 hour period each day. Several experts have different opinions but the general rule of thumb is to fast for 14 hours for women and 16 hours for men. During that period, you are only to have a maximum of 50 calories, which is basically 1 sugarless tea or coffee or perhaps half a piece of fruit or something similarly small.

How it helps with weight loss: By reducing your eating period to 8-10 hours each day, you are likely to eat less overall. Especially if are someone who would snack and consume beverages through the day. Some experts suggest the practice also speeds up your metabolism for when you do eat.

I have had no major (though perhaps minor) changes in energy or weight since I began the practice but others have. I was never overweight to begin with and I still eat the exact same amount as I did before, only now it is all consumed within 8 hours. The reason I do it is because a) I drink more water now (most people don't get enough water and hunger is often mistaken for thirst) and b) I have 16 hours a day where I am not distracted by food. My efficiency is ridiculously higher and the risk of falling into poor eating habits over 2/3 of my day is non-existent. I only have to think about food for 1/3 of it.

Some nutritionists over the years have suggested that the body can only absorb a certain amount of calories per hour and so larger meals are to be avoided. This is not the case. As long as you get your nutritional needs met each day, meal size is not an issue. For some people, larger meals can make you feel more sluggish for a period, so if that is the case, then you might want to have smaller meals. As for hunger, it has never been an issue. Sometimes I feel mild hunger, more so after about 14 hours, but a small sip of water always fixes it.

Take the Principle

I know intermittent fasting will not be for everyone. The point is to utilize the principle. I usually eat between 1pm and 9pm. I have a late lunch, an even later breakfast and all my other meals in that period. Sometimes I have a dessert treat too. What I don't do is snack, especially during those key winding down periods for sleep. If you don't want to do it fully, it is still a great rule not to eat after dinner in order to not interfere with your sleep cycle. Everyone should have at least a 10-hour gap within each 24-hour period (most of this to be taken up by sleep) where they do not eat and you can slowly increase the gap over time if you like.

Smoking, Alcohol and Recreational Drug Consumption

- **Smoking:** It introduces poisonous toxins into the body; it can be extremely harmful and has no health benefits.
- **Alcohol:** Even in moderation, it is never healthy. It is a treat. What about wine? Wine is not healthy. Athletes do not drink wine in the days before competing. Yes, wine has antioxidants, but there are other ways to get them without wine and without the risk of over-consumption or addiction. Alcohol in moderation is a treat and regular use is usually best avoided.
- **Recreational Drug Use:** All regular recreational drug use interferes with brain and metabolic processing. Learning impairment and unhealthy changes in weight and sleep are common. Both over-consumption of alcohol and recreational drug use (and in some ways smoking as well) severely increase the risk of mental illness and are common in depressive, anxious and other disorders.

Principle Summary

New You Nutrition: Lose weight, stop emotional eating and avoid the latest diets and weight loss scams by uncovering how to eat without obsession.

Study an elite athlete if you really want to understand what healthy eating is. Drink plenty of water, and reduce saturated fats, sugar and salt. Most of your diet should be made up of lean protein and vegetables and avoid pre-packaged foods in preference of fresh whole foods. Use ARE to slowly modify your diet and aim to not eat at all a minimum of 10 hours a day.

Fast-Action Techniques

1. Implement ARE immediately. Review your regular eating habits and make a healthy dietary addition, replacement and elimination today. Then do the next cycle and so on once you have adjusted to the most recent changes.
2. Consider the intermittent fasting principle and at what level it should be applied to your life. Determine which parts of your day in particular should be water only and make sure you always have access to water in general.
3. Plan your meals in terms of how you will approach them environmentally and mentally. Use this chapter's food guidelines in terms of food selection and preparation and how you shop and stock your home. If seeking weight reduction, drink water first, reduce food on plate by 20% and accept any cravings or ravenous emotions. They will pass (and become less frequent over time) as you proceed to eat mindfully, one enjoyable bite at a time.

Hypnotic Recording – Rapid Weight Loss Re-set: For guided assistance in moving beyond the principles and techniques of this chapter, a guided brain re-training process to assist you in rapidly moving towards a healthy goal weight and developing new, healthy and sustainable food related behaviors is available now at - http://mentalhealthhypnosis.com/weightloss

Other related Hypnotic Recordings – Quitting Toxic Habits: For guided assistance in moving beyond the principles and techniques of this chapter, guided brain re-training processes to assist you in quitting smoking, alcohol or recreational drug use are available at these links:

http://mentalhealthhypnosis.com/quitsmoking
http://mentalhealthhypnosis.com/quitdrinking
http://mentalhealthhypnosis.com/quitdrugs

Deep Sound Sleep
Establish new sleep hygiene habits to maximize your rest and daily energy

Welcome to the world of the "living dead." Wherever you go, stimulant jacked up "zombies" running on fumes have you surrounded and could cause catastrophic harm. These "zombies" pose a real threat to your safety, but the risk is not one of aggression but of accident proneness. If you wish to survive the "zombie apocalypse" first look into the mirror. Do you have red eyes with puffy lids and dark circles, pale skin, shallow breath, a droopy mouth and a hanging head? You may have already been infected but fortunately it is not too late. You can still be saved.

Modern society has somehow forgotten just how vital deep, rejuvenating, restful sleep is. In fact when people are struggling with stress or most types of mental illness, sleep disturbance is very often one of the core problems. Fatigue (often caused by sleep deprivation) is the number one cause of road and workplace accidents.

Good sleep often requires a routine that prepares the mind and the body the right way for sleep. Just like you should prepare your work environment for optimal performance, it is critical that you also follow key principles to develop sound sleeping patterns. You need to prepare your mental and physical environment for sleep. Although there are some people that can go to sleep almost at any time with very little effort, there are many others who really struggle.

On the mental side, sleep disturbance occurs most often because people are feeling stressed and unable to let go of their worries and concerns. On the physical side, poor sleep is mostly related to poor bed time practices. Environmental modifications are where we will begin.

The first rule is to make your room as dark and as quiet as possible and it tends to help if it is slightly cool. Having a window open at least a little also allows fresh air to circulate and tends to increase comfort. At least half an hour before bed, reduce light exposure.

Use low light emitting lamps or a dimmer switch if you have one. You are starting to tell your body that it is time to start winding down. What this means is also avoid using big bright lights, like the bathroom light, directly before bed. All your major night-time procedures like brushing your teeth should be done at least half an hour before bed, or if feasible, in low light.

The next major issue are your devices. The half hour rule applies here too. Don't bring your phone, tablet, or laptop to bed as these are all highly stimulating devices. They can also cause distractions, interruptions and highly irritating buzzes and jingles. There should be no television for at least half an hour before bed and you should definitely avoid watching television in bed.

Bed Activities

Your bed should be for sleep and sex only. The only other possibly acceptable activity might be some easy reading by lamplight for a short period of time before retiring. Once you start watching television in bed, eating, working in bed and so on, you start to confuse the mind as to the purpose of the bed. It starts to move away from being a clear trigger for sleep.

The Body Clock

Abundant amounts of research have demonstrated that we have a body clock. We are supposed to go to bed when it is dark and awaken with the increasing of light. This reality can make it very difficult for shift workers and travellers. Although imperfect, the same rules apply. If you need to sleep during the day, make your room as dark as you can and if possible, aim to simulate gentle light starting to gain in intensity over a half hour period as it is time to wake. One possible way to accomplish this is with specialized lamps that have that feature that simulate gradual increasing of light like a sunrise.

Amount: Few people ever seem to agree on how much sleep they should have. Based on general guidelines and my experience with assisting others, unless somehow superhuman, 6 hours is the bare minimum you should have. 7 hours seems to work well for many and 8 hours has always been the general belief and is fine too.

The issue with 8 hours is, of course, in today's busy world, people struggle with setting aside that much time and it may not be necessary either. Unless a teenager, any more than 8 hours and you run the risk of oversleeping and suffering with additional fatigue during the day. Teenagers, due to their rapid growth can have up to 9 hours and for most, they tend to have a cycle where they are most alert later in the evening and would benefit from getting up later in the day. This of course is not always possible. However, I have come across High Schools where students start around 11am and finish around 5pm and those students tend to be more productive, happier and enjoy school more.

Trying to trick the system: Some people believe in the idea of playing 'catch-up' sleep on the weekends. This is not advisable. The occasional sleep in after a hectic week may be okay, but the sleep cycle generally craves consistency through the whole week. One of the reasons a lot of people tend to hate Mondays is because they are feeling groggy after two days of an altered sleep cycle.

Establishing a New Routine

When creating a new routine, there is only one thing you can control and that is the wake up time. Therefore, it is important to set the same wake up time for each day and work backwards from there.

Example: Assuming you have set a time for 7a.m., and the goal is 8 hours, then you should be in bed at 11p.m and winding down by at least 10:30p.m.

The rules for training a new cycle: For those who have trouble getting to sleep, this is critical. Even though the goal is for 11p.m. bedtime, initially you will not go to bed until you are sleepy. If you are not sleepy until 2a.m. do not go to bed until that time. With each successive night as you crave more sleep, you should start to feel sleepier earlier and you can work your way backwards to the 11p.m. bedtime goal. Once set, aim to maintain it during the whole week.

Waking up: Knowing that the bed is for sleep and sex only, what should you do if you are struggling to get to sleep or waking up for extended periods during the night? Don't stay in bed. If you can't fall asleep after 20 minutes, leave the bed but avoid all major stimulation. Remain under low to no light and do a simple task only. Easy reading, light cleaning, any task you find boring or mindfulness practice are good options. Only return to bed when you are sleepy. If you return and after 20 minutes you are struggling to sleep again, do the same thing again.

At first, this can be difficult, but because you will get up at the same time each day, your body is going to crave catching up on sleep with each additional night.

Naps: I love naps, but for sleep strugglers, I tend to not recommend them. If you are someone who struggles to get to sleep at night, one reason may be because a nap is interfering with your sleep cycle. In this case, avoid napping so the additional fatigue is more likely to assist you to want to sleep at the right time at night.

If getting to sleep is not an issue, and your body is comfortable with naps, one or two 20-30 minute naps can offer a great system recharge and help you problem solve. One of the great benefits of naps, is if you are struggling with a problem and are able to calm yourself enough to have a nap, your unconscious mind is likely to work on that problem for you as you sleep and you are much more likely to find a suitable answer to it when you awaken. If napping is not for you, mindfulness practice can act as a good substitute.

Food: Some research suggests there are certain foods that assist with sleep. I believe it is not worth the risk. Considering so many people struggle with diet, the last thing I would recommend is having anything other than water after dinner and during the rest of the night time hours. Food will stimulate your system, especially anything with sugar will cause a spike, and so it is best avoided. Depending on how it affects you, I would suggest no coffee (and of course no energy drinks, which are horrible and you should not drink at all) after 2p.m., but possibly even earlier.

Alcohol, drug or cigarette reduction or avoidance later in the day is also advisable. Many people fall into the trap of using alcohol as a sleep enabler. Alcohol acts a sedative similar to sedative medications; regular use will create unwanted side effects and is likely to create dependency and interfere with your natural sleep cycle.

Dealing with Stress and Worry

I meet so many people who struggle to wind down because they can't seem to let go of their daily concerns at bedtime. Practicing mindfulness before bed is often a great solution to this. It also is good to do if you wake up during the night within that 20-minute period before you should leave the bed if you don't fall back asleep.

Another good strategy is to write down all the things on your mind before bed, knowing that they will be there in the morning and you will be able to better deal with them then after a night of rest, where your unconscious mind will work to solve them. What happens if you wake up in the middle of the night with an idea or because of something you need to address? One option is to have a large notepad and just write out the basic idea in the dark (or with very low light), then go back to sleep. Another is to trust your unconscious mind that, if it is important, the idea will return when you are awake.

Importance and purpose: Sleep-deprived people are dangerous! Fatigue is one of the highest causes for car and workplace accidents. It leads to poorer memory, judgment, irritability and impulsiveness. With the increased stress on the body, your immunity goes down and you are at a much higher risk of illness. One study has shown those getting five or less hours of sleep are 50% more likely to be overweight.

In terms of mental illness, depression, bipolar disorder and schizophrenia in particular are very often preceded with a sleep disorder. The same genes that are affected by poor sleep are the same genes affected by mental illness. Getting your sleep right is essential for good mental health.

Sleep provides a critical function. It actually allows for learning and memory to solidify and stabilize during the night and enhances your creativity. Attention, concentration, decision making, mood management and overall health are all enhanced when getting enough sleep.

Principle Summary

Deep Sound Sleep: Establish new sleep hygiene habits to maximize your rest and daily energy.

Follow a consistent and calming sleep ritual. Keep to the same sleep times, reduce mental stimulation and work to clear your mind before bed. Trust in your unconscious mind to solve any additional left over problems of the day while you sleep.

Fast-Action Techniques

1. Set a consistent wake up time and work backwards from there towards a suitable bed time in order to establish a healthy new pattern.
2. Place a notepad next to your bed so you can write out any problems or concerns you have before bed. Also write down if you like at the end of your list "I will now trust in my unconscious mind to work through these problems as I sleep soundly tonight in order to have a fresh perspective in the morning."
3. Remove all sleep distractions and interference habits. Make sure you wind down before bed and that the bed is used for sleep and sex only.

Hypnotic Recording – Sleep Soundly: For guided assistance in moving beyond the principles and techniques of this chapter, a guided brain re-training process to assist you in establishing a strong sleep trigger, a healthy and regular pattern, more positive and solution focused dreams and greater time in deep sleep is available now at this link - http://mentalhealthhypnosis.com/sleep

Part 3: The Principles of Meaningful Living

Expose Yourself to Overcome Fear and Anxiety
Exposure is the most scientifically proven method for curing fears, phobias, panic and generalized anxiety issues

To have a successful life you must learn to overcome anxiety and fear. To overcome fear and anxiety, you have to put yourself in a position of vulnerability. You have to face it, fully and openly. You have to expose yourself to it. You need to get naked!

You've got two options. You can look it square in the eye and tear your clothes off and shock it and yourself until it backs away. Or, you can seduce it, and flirt with it, stripping off one piece of clothing at a time until you are completely exposed. At first it's scary, but by the end you will be liberated, naked and free and ready to dance with it.

I am going to reveal the two most scientifically researched and proven ways to reduce anxiety and overcome fear. They both involve you facing your fear. All meaningful living requires fear to be faced. One method is highly confronting and terrifying. It is the psychological equivalent of "tearing" your clothes off in front of all the people you would least like to see you naked and staying there, perhaps for hours, until they left. It is called flooding.

Let's assume you are deathly afraid of snakes. All I have to do is lock you in a room full of snakes AND NOT LET YOU OUT until your fear goes away. No matter what you do, I don't let you out. You might have a panic attack or two and pass out. I still won't let you out. You might scream, plead and beg to be released, but I won't let you out. You are not let out until I can see you have adjusted and no longer fear the snakes. It could take up to several hours and it would feel awful.

The other method works on the same principle, but is much more humane. It is called "graded exposure" and is the equivalent of slowly "stripping" your clothes off and adjusting to each level of clothing removal before proceeding. I'll use overcoming a fear of public speaking to illustrate how this amended process works.

There is a guaranteed way to overcome fear. It is called habituation which can be explained as a gradual reduction to your sensitivity to anything new or out of your normal comfort zone. The more unusual the experience, the more intensely the fear is felt. Your heart rate increases, your muscles become tenser and your breathing becomes shallower to name a few natural physiological changes. Your thoughts become more catastrophic and you will feel anxious. This is a sign of alertness and an enhanced ability to escape from potential danger. The more different the environment is to the one you are used to, the more aroused you will be.

If you do not understand the process of exposure, you may be unknowingly training yourself to be afraid. As I said, I will use the example of public speaking. Graph 1, on the next page, indicates that as your anxiety reached a certain level, you found a way to escape the situation(indicated by the arrow pointing to the left) and so your anxiety drops back down to 0 or close to 0 (indicated by the dotted arrow pointing downwards) as you avoid the anxiety provoking experience. Unfortunately, for you, though, this speech is important and needs to be made.

The next time you are in the same or similar situation, so in this example when it comes time to make the speech again, your level of anxiety will jump up very quickly to the point it was before you last escaped. That is basically where you level of anxious arousal will be starting from and it will continue to rise.

Let's say that as it begins rising again (Graph 2), you once again find a way to escape the situation. In the short term, that is great, as your anxiety again reduces to 0 or close to it. But, now, you have trained your anxiety to basically begin from the level it was at when you escaped the second time and that is where you will basically be starting on your third attempt (Graph 3) and it will continue to rise.

The only option, in regards to overcoming this fear, is to face it correctly, by adhering to two key principles.

Expose Yourself to Overcome Fear and Anxiety

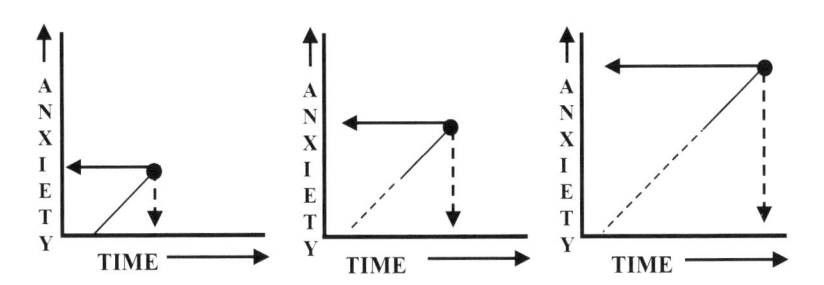

77

There are two principles when it comes to this process of facing your fear, otherwise known as exposure. It is the <u>Amount of total exposures</u> and <u>Length of each exposure</u>.

That is how often you are exposed to your fear, also known as frequency (the more times the better), and for how long you face that fear each time, also known as duration (and the longer this occurs the better).

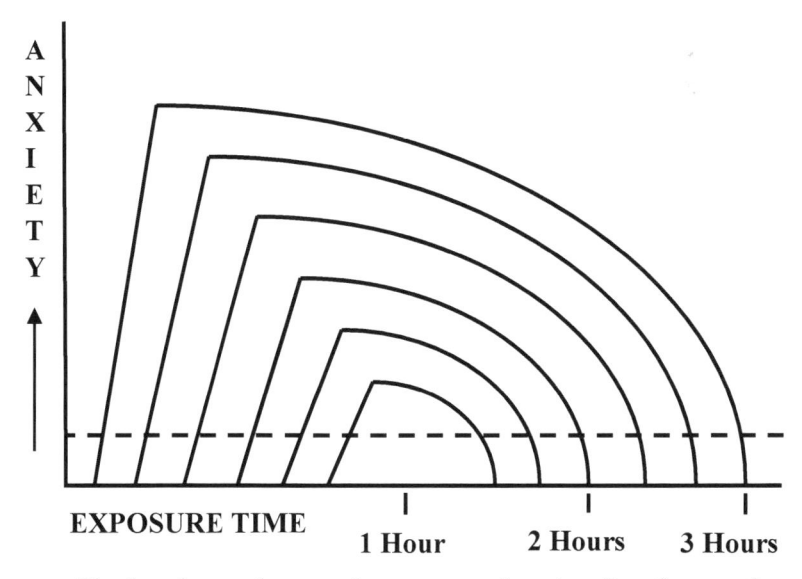

The key is you have to been exposed to that fear frequently and for a long enough period of time, on each occasion, for your fear to reduce. This is called habituating. I added a dotted line across the graph below to indicate that your level of anxiety will not always start at 0 or habituate completely, but over time it can start from and return to a mild and manageable level.

There may be several challenges per experience. You may have to overcome several smaller fears first before attempting the larger one. Each challenge has its own exposure curve. In anything you have ever learnt or done, the principle of exposure was present. Learning to walk, or ride a bicycle or drive a car. Going to school for the first time, or first day on the job and meeting new people all initially increase arousal and require habituation over time to occur.

Imagine if you never went to school because you were afraid on that first day. How dull would your life be and how much would you miss out? Every time you face and overcome a fear, your life expands and more interesting experiences become available. Every time you avoid an experience, your life contracts. This is not necessarily bad as not everybody needs to be a public speaker or deal with snakes. However, what if your dream job became available but you knew speaking would be part of it? Or, you find your dream home but it's in an area with snakes. Now you have a reason to overcome your fear.

As you know, behaviour is king and in the main example, we have been referring to a physical act, that of public streaking – I mean speaking. However, the exposure principles relate to every aspect of your experience (thoughts, images, memories, emotions, sensations, and urges) too.

Other Forms of Exposure

Internal exposure: The way you deal with all the things that happen inside of you when anxious and fearful is by practicing mindful acceptance (previously addressed in "Mindful Acceptance" chapter). As you expose yourself physically by acting towards your goal, you will also have numerous internal fear experiences. The aim is to notice, accept, and let go of those internal experiences as you continue to physically move towards your goal. However, no matter what you think and feel, if you physically expose yourself correctly, all elements of the fear will reduce.

Knowing how to best deal with your internal experience simply makes the whole process a lot easier. If your internal experience was not of concern, then we wouldn't need *graded exposure* and I would just *flood* you every time. Mindful acceptance and mental focus principles are of course important and have been addressed in other chapters.

Exposure through imagination: What happens if you physically cannot expose yourself to a fear in any practical way? You simply do not have the opportunity to practice public speaking before the big speech, or you're afraid of flying? The same principle applies; it is just done through imagination. The key is making the scenarios in your mind as vivid and real as possible. The more realistic the imagined exposure, the faster habituation will happen.

You must follow the same principles within reason. If your speech is to go for an hour, you may need to have several regular 20-30 minute exposures to get ready. You end each exposure when you reach a comfortable level. The same principle applies with flying. You wouldn't actually need to do a 16-hour imagined exposure to prepare for a 16-hour flight.

Exposure and positive experiences (Over-Exposure): Up until this point, we have been discussing exposure in relation to overcoming fear. However, habituation (the reduction of the intensity of an experience as exposed over time) relates to all experiences. In simple words, too much of a good thing will kill the buzz. Some of this happens naturally and some of it is important to control.

Whenever you buy a new television, or car, or home, at first, because it is new and different and more advanced than the previous model, it's exciting and there is a boost in pleasure. However, over time, due to continual use (exposure), the additional pleasure wears off and once again, the "new car" simply becomes "the car" and so on. So after a while in search of a new buzz, people will once again change their car, television and so on. Once again the effects are likely to be temporary.

The best way to keep life interesting and avoid over-exposure and thus boredom is to continually have a good dose of variety.

However, rather than new things, what is usually more effective are more varied experiences, as they are more unpredictable. Holidays to new locations, meeting new people and learning new courses and other creative pursuits are all great options. Use the pure pleasures and authentic achievement principles to assist you to make life more interesting and enjoyable.

Principle Summary

Expose Yourself to Overcome Fear and Anxiety: The most scientifically proven method for curing fears, phobias, panic and generalized anxiety issues.

The more often and the longer the period of time you spend facing and accepting your fear, the more control you will gain over it as its intensity will reduce (habituation). You can start slowly and cautiously as long as you continue to increase exposures over time.

Fast-Action Techniques

1. Choose a small fear and separate its components into small sub-goals. Start with the easiest sub-goal and slowly build your way up from there. You must regularly expose yourself to the fear and for a long enough period each time before moving on to the next goal. Once you are confident about overcoming smaller fears, use the same principles to go after larger ones. For example, if you had a fear of snakes, you could complete the following set of exposures. You may start by looking at a picture of a snake, then watching a video, then holding a toy snake, then visiting one in a cage, then touching it and eventually holding it.
2. Add more variety in your life to avoid boredom-based habituation. Consider three activities you regularly do that have started to become boring and incorporate new modifications to the activity to make it more interesting.
3. Do a set of imagined exposures for a fear you may not be able to easily practice exposing to yourself physically such as flying. Break it up the same way as the snakes example above.

Aim to remain mindfully accepting of your feelings through the whole exposure process (whether physical or imagined) and aim to keep your breathing deep and regular.

Hypnotic Recording – The General Anxiety and High Stress Solution: For guided assistance in moving beyond the principles and techniques of this chapter, a guided brain re-training process to assist you in knowing how to trigger deep calmness, enhance environmental safety awareness, re-set your anxiety mechanism to be a more relaxed person and increase self-assuredness is at - http://mentalhealthhypnosis.com/anxietyandstress

Hypnotic Recording – Freedom from Fear and Phobia: For guided assistance in moving beyond the principles and techniques of this chapter, a guided brain re-training process to assist you in knowing how to create an automatic calmness trigger, correctly and safely expose yourself to overcome a specific fear or phobia, and feel empowered to successfully face any difficult situation is at - http://mentalhealthhypnosis.com/fearandphobia

Cycles of Life
Understand what is required to successfully recover from grief, bereavement, trauma and loss

People can be cruel and deeply insensitive. It's not always intentional, often it's not, but the effect of the comment still hurts. Have you have ever lost someone or something long ago and were feeling the pain of that loss but felt scared or ashamed to mention it? Even though you may want to reach out, you're afraid of receiving a response like this:

"Haven't you gotten over that yet?!"

Clearly the answer is "no!" It's also a foolish assumption because in some ways we never completely "get over" anything. To "get over" a painful event implies once you overcome that hurdle, there will be no others and you'll never look back. But as you know by now, you can't control every thought or feeling you have. It also illustrates the problem with one of our greatest illusions, that of time being linear.

Calendars, graphs, and digital clocks suggest time is linear. However, there is no indication of this in nature. The Earth orbits the sun and rotates to create day and night and the seasons. All these events remain consistent over time. Therefore nature and time are not linear, but cyclical. We actually do spend our entire life, going around in circles.

More than anything else, our triggers, whether positive or negative are based on where we are in a particular cycle. What does the first day of Spring remind you of, probably the first day of Spring in years past and everything to do with Spring in general. What the first day of Spring is not likely to remind you of is that period a third of the way into Winter. You may not think about certain things in years until a cyclical trigger brings it back.

For example, an alcoholic may have been sober and avoidant of pubs for 20 years until one day he or she decides to journey into the pub during a winter reunion with old friends. Instantly numerous pleasurable triggers activate (especially because no non-drinking exposures in pubs ever occurred – see "Expose Yourself"

Chapter) and so he or she thinks "it's okay to have just one," and then maybe another and then suddenly the old dormant drinking cycle is suddenly brought back to life.

(Another issue here is that of identity as many "alcoholics" are taught to always view themselves as reforming alcoholics as opposed to becoming "non-drinkers." When working on a large issue like addiction, it is important to move beyond the behavior and towards the changing of identity. These issues are addressed in the Self-Image Chapter.)

Cycles of human pain and pleasure: Most of us will start to feel more and more excited in the time leading up to birthdays and holidays and cycle more towards sadness and reflection in the time towards anniversaries of death and loss. However with each additional extended exposure (see Exposure Principle) to an experience, its intensity will weaken. In terms of positive events, it is important to add variety to keep it interesting and in terms of painful events, it is vital to practice mindful acceptance (which also acts as a psychological exposure), move towards calmness and seek lessons from the experience. Learning is also cyclical as we *regularly need to repeat and further develop lessons already learnt as we cycle through life.*

The Infinity Cycle

I will illustrate the life cycles principle through my own modification of the infinity symbol.

Life without learning or growth could be represented by a circle. As you move through each cycle, the same triggers occur and the intensity of your responses remains the same over time.

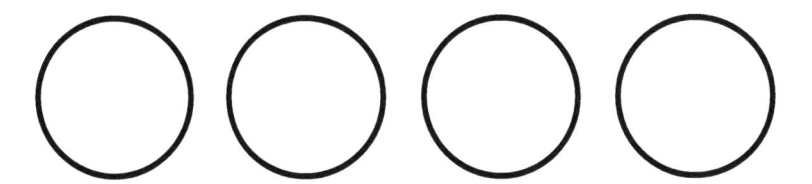

The 4 Infinity Cycle Figures: Exploring a Painful Experience

On the next page are the infinity cycles. In the initial cycles, the pain and hurt will be intense and periods of positive coping and adaptation are shorter.

The arrows represent the progression of time in each cycle and the bolded arrow represents the starting point after the trigger.

As you progress through each cycle over time your ability to cope and adapt increases due to natural life exposure and other coping skills you may learn. However, when triggers occur, some pain and hurt will still be felt regardless of how long ago the initial painful event was experienced.

Important note on severe trauma: The exact same principle applies, however because experiences tend to be very intense, the sufferer will usually work even harder to avoid them, therefore natural and lengthy exposures will be much rarer and the healing process via natural exposure alone over time would be extremely slow. Furthermore, avoidance attempts through unhealthy habits like poorer diet, reduced exercise, social withdrawal, drug and alcohol abuse and so on will make natural healing without professional intervention even more difficult.

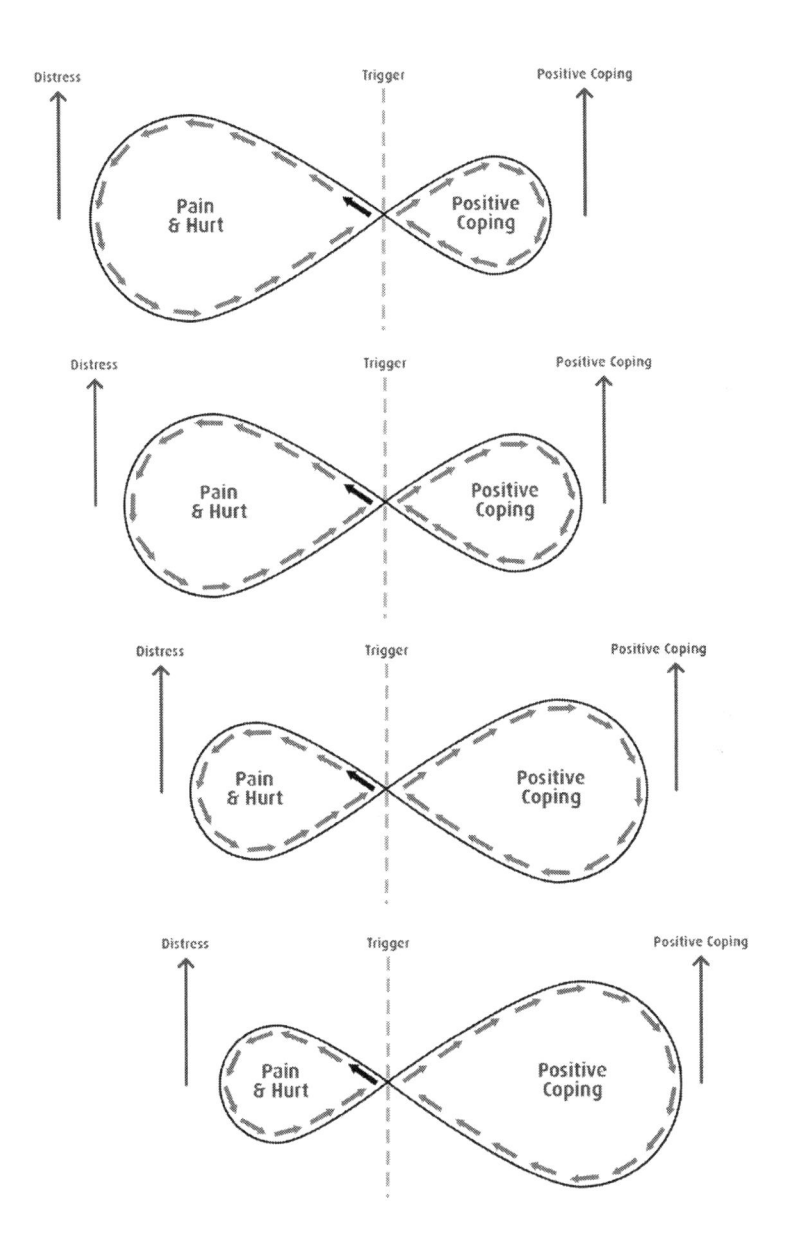

Dealing with Pain, Hurt, Loss and Grief

Life is painful! It is pleasurable too. Both are part of life and both can never be completely "gotten over." The classic phrase "time heals" is not completely true. Correctly completed exposures over time heal but pain is never completely eliminated. Additionally, depending on where in a cycle you are, some triggers will be more intense than others.

Now you understand how damaging and insensitive a comment like "that was years ago, get over it" is. Too many times as a therapist I've heard people make that comment about themselves. "Shouldn't I be over this?" Nothing is ever completely over, and that is part of the secret in knowing how to deal with the pain of life.

If you examine a positive experience, you can also understand how stupid and unrealistic the comment is. When you have an adult friend recalling the events of a fun childhood experience like a birthday party, do you respond with "that was years ago, get over it!" Perhaps only if they were constantly talking about it, and even then, that wouldn't be the best way to inspire them to change topics.

Knowing that life and progress is not completely linear, but cyclical, here are five key rules to keep in mind.

Rule 1: Avoid "beating yourself up" when you experience the return of difficult thoughts and emotions in relation to tough experiences.

Rule 2: Accept (the elephant) that it is there. Mindfully observe the experience, explore your thoughts and feelings without believing that is who you are or that you need to follow them. Gently expose yourself (think "strip" not "tear") to the experience. Let it cycle through you and be as accepting as possible. Whatever you feel or think is fine. If tears or shivers or other sensations come, let them come.

Rule 3: Seek lessons so you can better adapt to related experiences in the future. Every experience has lessons attached to it and some may need repeating and further development. Like the wisdom of the elephant, they are not always immediately obvious.

Perhaps the lesson is to be safer in the future and avoid such dangerous situations. Maybe it's that you need to show greater appreciation for what you have, whilst you still have it. Or, follow an impulse to learn a new skill and so on. Be open to whatever comes.

Rule 4: Find patient support. If no one you trust is available, still aim to be supportive and patiently encouraging of yourself as you process the experience and seek lessons. You may not always get the lessons immediately. If you wish to discuss the experience with someone else, make sure it is someone you trust, a person who is kind, compassionate, patient and non-judgmental.

Rule 5: Remind yourself that you are experiencing something that is part of a cycle. Cycles never change but your ability to cope with them can improve. Pain is natural and normal and, with acceptance, you will soon pass through it to a different part of the cycle. After the Winter, there is always Spring.

The completion of a cycle in life is called a revolution. Revolution can also mean a major change to a type of system. By working through painful experiences in a mindfully accepting manner and seeking the lessons, you may find yourself achieving both kinds of revolution.

Principle Summary

Cycles of Life: Understand what is required to successfully recover from grief, bereavement, trauma and loss.

Time and progression through life is not linear but cyclical. What will trigger you will depend on where you are in a cycle and you will need to repeat and further develop lessons already learnt as you cycle through life. You will never fully "get over" some events but you can accept and learn from each reminder.

Fast-Action Techniques

1. Recall a difficult life experience you have had. Go back and view the event again in your mind and aim to remain as neutral and accepting as possible. Once the event is over, seek three important life lessons to take from having experienced that event.

2. Imagine a future scenario (or one current if relevant) where a close friend has to deal with a difficult life period. Envision yourself being a highly supportive and empathic friend. Notice how you act and speak and what you say and write down what you learn from this exercise.
3. Consider a difficult experience you know you will face in the future, such as the loss of a loved one, and imagine working through the five rules for overcoming loss until you get to an emotionally satisfactory and healthy place. Write down what you learn.

Hypnotic Recording – Overcoming Grief or Loss: For guided assistance in moving beyond the principles and techniques of this chapter, a guided brain re-training process to assist you in coping with grief or loss (e.g. loss of a loved one, a relationship or friend, a pet, a job or dealing with injury etc.) and finding empowering lessons and new inspiration from those difficult experiences is available at - http://mentalhealthhypnosis.com/grieforloss

Praise Pays
Successfully share the most essential human need and actively love yourself

You were once totally helpless. As a baby, you were completely at the mercy of others. Fortunately, despite the imperfections of our caregivers, almost all of us will be raised in loving and nurturing environments. Unfortunately, some babies will be abused. There are actually two types of abuse. There is the obvious form, assault, where clear physical evidence of harm is witnessed, and then there is the other type which is also extremely dangerous. What makes the second type so horrifying is that a good natured person may frequently participate in this kind of abuse and not even realize it.

I want you to imagine that you are a baby being raised in an orphanage. However, be aware that this is a very unique orphanage. Your caregivers are given special instructions. Their instructions are to take care of you as required and as efficiently as possible. What this means is you will be fed, clothed, bathed, changed and kept warm as required. Knowing that all these needs will be taken care of, how do you feel? *Is there anything missing? Before continuing, really think about it.*

What is missing is natural human interaction. The caregivers have been instructed to attend to your physical needs only. They do not play, hug, smile, encourage or engage in baby talk with you. They simply attend to your physical needs as required. Really consider this situation. *How does it feel? What do you foresee happening because of this?*

The answer is it will kill you! You may not actually die physically, but then again you may. If you do actually survive past infancy, you will suffer from severe emotional, psychological, intellectual and physical retardation. Your growth will be stunted, your ability to control your emotions and understand others debilitated and your intellectual functioning will be damaged.

This did happen. Many years ago, in select Romanian orphanages, caregivers were instructed to only care for the physical needs of the babies. A disproportionately large amount died in infancy and, of those that did not, many struggled with the other aforementioned problems for the rest of their shortened lives.

These babies died not because their caregivers did anything wrong, but because caregivers were instructed to go against their instincts and not to do enough right. Even though they were not treated badly, the babies suffered because they were not treated well. Without the babies experiencing the physical expression of their deepest need, which of course are demonstrations of love, they became afraid of life.

After all, without love, the world is a truly horrifying place and love is the greatest human growth catalyst known to man. If you think it is only babies who need constant love hits, you are wrong! It is a requirement for optimal living at all ages.

Full Circle – Revealing the Ultimate Pleasure

Praise is an act of love. It can be given to others, but it is also important that it be directed and received by the self. Kindness, encouragement, kudos, support, connecting, cheering, compliments and so on all fit into the category of praise and acts of love. The greater the intensity of the acts, the more love being expressed, and emotions are contagious so what you offer will tend to be returned. On the other hand, acts of criticism, spite, bullying, harm, neglect and hatred are all acts of fear. Once again, the more intense the expression is, the greater the fear and the deeper the cycle of conflict.

The Unfair Advantage

Choose any event and the principle I am about to illustrate will ring true. For simplicity sake, I am going to use a soccer match as an example. Imagine this scenario. It happens quite frequently. There are two teams; both are equal in players, skills and abilities. On this day, all the members of each team feel like they are on the top of their game and the referees are on top of theirs. Neither team has any particular skill or luck based advantage over the other and yet one team has a much greater chance of winning.

Which team has a greater chance of winning and why?

Really think about it.

If you need a clue, do not just think about what happens on the field.

The answer is the team with the home ground advantage. That will be the team with the most support. They will receive far more praise than the other team and far less criticism during the game. Even though the crowd is not actually playing, none of them ever get on the field or touch the ball, except for the occasional streaker, the effect is still undeniable. The home ground advantage is given so much weight that in many professional soccer competitions, if two teams play twice where one match is played at home and one away, and both times the score is equal, the team who scored more goals when playing away from home actually wins the encounter. Praise is a very real and very powerful force.

Pitch Perfect Praise

There are few things in life where perfection is possible. Offering or receiving praise in the right way can often lead to perfect moments. Praise is both a verbal and non-verbal process that is expressed through word selection, tone of voice and body language. For praise to be most effective, it must be pitched correctly. It is like a tiny presentation that requires all of the right elements to be accepted. There are only three simple elements you need to keep in mind to guide your praise. To stay on track, follow GPS.

The key components of a Pitch Perfect Praise are:

    Genuineness
    Presence
    Specificity

The first component is it has to be Genuine. You have to really mean it! Offering a half-hearted compliment will be received as an insult. If it is not genuine, don't do it! The next thing is you need to be Present. The first rule of presence is whatever you want them to feel, you first aim to generate that feeling inside yourself. Let's assume you want to present a feeling of kindness, openness and warmth. Now that you know what to feel, you can then present your praise. Smiling, obtaining eye contact, speaking clearly and keeping open body language if possible is a good way to do this.

The final component is often neglected and is the most important. Tell or show them specifically for what it is you are praising them. Of course, you can offer general praise, but being specific will make it much more powerful. Saying "you look nice," "good job," "nice work," and so on are okay, but they do not really offer enough feedback as to why you think that. To illustrate specificity, some examples are offered below.

"I really like the model you used to analyze these reports. You've done a great job simplifying it."

"I totally appreciate you giving up your break time to help me move that package yesterday."

"I was very impressed by the effort you put in to look professional with our associates at Monday's lunch."

"Hey buddy, nice work with the furniture choice; these colors are exciting. You've got taste."

"I really noticed and enjoyed the effort you put into the dinner you made, especially those potatoes, very, very nice."

"Babe, when you walked in the room the other day, you had such an enthusiastic smile that everyone was instantly intrigued to meet you, including me!"

Now that you have your GPS system to act as a guide, the next questions are how often should you praise and to whom. The answer is as often as many as is feasible and with as many people as possible.

One perceived roadblock you may be thinking about is: what if you do not like the person you are to engage with. The answer is it does not matter. *Praisers are not pleasers.* You do not have to like, acknowledge or accept the things others do that you dislike. Despite that, there is always something you can praise someone for whether you like them or not. Simply choose to praise them for the things with which you do agree. If anything, it will demonstrate how classy you really are.

The Magic Ratios: The Pat versus Slap Principle

What if there was a rule, a simple ratio that if adhered to guaranteed a transformation of your business, your relationships, and your life. Well, there is. Remember these ratios.

- *+2.9:1 minimum in business (Discovered by Marcial Losada)*
- *+5:1 minimum in relationships (Discovered by John Gottman)*
- *+13:1 maximum in business and relationships*
- *+1:10 what I call the slap face versus pat back principle*

These are positive to negative interaction ratios. It all started with John Gottman who is a relationships expert and became able to predict with 94% accuracy couples who would be together in three years just by observing them interact for 15 minutes.

What he found was a magic interaction ratio that needed to be adhered to for relationships to not just survive but grow. The ratio was 5:1 positive to negative interactions. For every negative interaction (criticism, contemptuous look or remark, rejection, irritable remark, etc.) there needed to be at least five positive interactions (specific praise, compliments, smiles, affectionate touches, etc.) for the relationship to work. Less than this and failure was almost guaranteed. In business, the same principle applies with a minimum of 3:1 to avoid unnecessary workplace conflict and reductions in productivity.

At the same time, there is a maximum, which appears to be about 13:1. What this means is our relationships should not always be completely positive. That would fall into the realm of pleasing which would reduce healthy critical questioning essential for growth. That being said, you can still be critical when required without being harsh. Elegant communication is discussed in the relationships chapter.

Finally there is 1:10, which suggests that a piece of criticism may have up to 10 times the negative impact on someone as a piece of praise. If you recall, we have a bias towards protection and pain avoidance and therefore we will remember negative events more easily, and feel them more deeply. An easy way to think of it is a slap in the face is 10 times more powerful than a pat on the back.

What all this leads to is knowing that we need to minimise unnecessary and inelegant criticism and maximize praise to be psychologically healthy. Ignoring people is a form of neglect and also a type of criticism. For confidence and happiness to grow we must express praise. Love always takes a lot more work to build and sustain than fear. Without it you will start to die and so will those around you. Practice using GPS based praise as frequently as possible and your confidence and the impact you have on others will transform. However, it is also essential that you dedicate yourself to the practice of self-praise.

Self-Praise

The small acts of love that you express to others you must also direct towards yourself. How often do you take the time to get present, find a specific act you did well and genuinely praise yourself for it? My guess is rarely. In looking after others, we often neglect ourselves, and neglect is also a form of punishment. As much as we thrive on acknowledgement from others, although not ideal, as adults we can still grow without it as long as we regularly praise ourselves.

Principle Summary

Praise Pays: Successfully share the most essential human need and actively love yourself.

GPS praise offerings are simple and tangible acts of love. As long as you still work to address actual problems, you can never give too much praise to yourself and others. *When in doubt, offer praise, it always pays!*

Fast-Action Techniques

1. Choose 1-3 times each day to go through this very short but powerful exercise.
    - Straighten your posture, start breathing deeply and close your eyes if you wish. Imagine stepping out of your body and looking back at yourself as you are now. As you look at yourself, you will follow the GPS formula by looking at yourself with genuine care and presence and you will mention 1-3 good things you have done recently. Aim to really feel the meaning of those words of acknowledgement, the sounds of your encouraging voice and any other sensory experiences that surface. As you do this, you will also show care through non-verbal actions such as patting yourself on the back, looking yourself in the eyes, projecting love, or giving yourself a hug. (You can verbalize and physicalize these actions in the real world if you want as well).
    - Then imagine stepping back inside your body, come back into the room and write down the self-praise given and keep it in a highly visible place so that you can read it again to give yourself as a confidence boost at any point in the day. Self-praise could look something like this. "I know I'm doing so well now because I have finished the first two chapters of my report. I feel really good knowing my great report will be completed by 5p.m. today and I will begin the next chapter immediately."
2. Choose 1-3 people who you have regular contact with and set a goal to notice praiseworthy behavior more often over the week. Offer each at least three GPS pieces of praise per day.
3. Select one person this week and choose a time to offer a "praise pounding." If you have children, you also have to do it with an adult. Reflect on at least 10 praiseworthy aspects of that person and offer at least five pieces of praise one after the other. This can be an absolutely wonderful experience. For

example, "You're so precise with the spices in your tasty cooking. I am so impressed how you have reached conversational level with your new language study. You started working out and have become at least 10% fitter in the last year. You're so patient with the kids. You care about cleanliness and even sometimes pick up other people's rubbish. You will dance without music. It's just so great to be around you."

Hypnotic Recording – The Praise Machine: For guided assistance in moving beyond the principles and techniques of this chapter, a guided brain re-training process to assist you in making GPS praise a more natural, easy and automatic process where you become more kind, loving, attentive and positively influential towards yourself and others is available now at the following link - http://mentalhealthhypnosis.com/praisemachine

Gratitude

Gratitude and giving are necessary practices and invaluable antidotes to greed, doubt, entitlement and other human pitfalls

Have you met the Joneses? I know you have heard of them but they are hard to keep up with. They are your lifelong neighbours. Wherever you go, the Joneses have already been and did it in greater style. Whatever you want, the Joneses already have and more. Everyone you know is just a fraction of who the Joneses know and have charmed. The Joneses have a bigger home, more gadgets, longer holidays, better jobs and smarter children.

The Joneses are everywhere! You never spend any time with them in person, but you can't escape them. They are on the television and radio, at your workplace and in your meetings, at the shops and at your children's parties. They even find a place at your dinner table and a way into your dreams at night.

The Joneses are an idea, an idea that you will never have enough, and they are ruining your life. But, it gets worse. The Joneses are ruining everyone's life because they promote two kinds of fantasy. One is if you have what they have, you will be happier. The second is you should be able to have what they have for virtually nothing.

Entitlement

We are in a world of entitlement. Everybody wants something for nothing and they often think they can get it. But, what they get has little to no value, for things of great value are not free. **All worthwhile things come with a cost. Usually the cost is time, energy and money.**

The world economy is a mess because of an entitlement mentality. It is based on people trying to have more than they deserve. And the saddest part was having these extra material things did not make people richer, but poorer because they became slaves to the very objects and ideals that were supposed to make life easier and more enjoyable.

No matter what your financial situation at present, it is essential that you be grateful for what you do have. Considering over 70% of the world lives on less than $2 a day, you have a lot. However, that does not mean that you are not eligible to receive more than you'll ever need. **You can have it all, but it can't come from a place of entitlement. Those who feel strong levels of entitlement tend to become angry quickly when they lose what they believe they deserve, even though they may have contributed nothing of value to earn it.** They fear that they cannot survive without the comforts that they have become accustomed.

What do you actually need? I can think of a handful and three of them are free: eat (drink), breathe, move and sleep. Basic clothing and shelter and of course acts of praise (love) help as well. Everything else is a luxury. This is so important that it deserves repeating.

EVERYTHING ELSE IS A LUXURY!

Almost every person in a western country has a television, washing machine, phone, fridge, computer, instant access to electricity and instant multiple faucet fresh water. Not even the wealthiest person on the planet had any of these things 150 years ago. For those that actually find a way to lose access to all these luxuries and more, apart from a catastrophic event, it is usually because of unloving and undisciplined experiences that have led to poor choices and debilitating addictions. However, even for all those people that truly do fall on hard times, access to all those key luxuries are still usually available.

The Purpose of Gratitude

If most of what you and I have is a luxury (think about the internet, with all the incredible information, audios and videos, with most of it being free or accessible for a fraction of what it would have cost pre-internet), why are so many people unhappy? The reason is because we habituate (see Exposure Principles) and so with regular continuous use the excitement created by the new product starts to reduce until it is just another thing. Unless we actively appreciate and experience in new ways what we do have, the enjoyment starts to wear off and we take it for granted.

However, it gets worse. Habituation does not just relate to objects, it relates to all aspects of your life. It is very easy to ignore or forget to actively appreciate your friends, family, job, yourself and the amazing experiences available to you in the past, present and future. Although it is fair to say that none of our friends, work and usual experiences are perfect, there are truly wonderful elements to be found and highlighted in all aspects of our life.

The regular practice of gratitude allows you to find, appreciate and enjoy those wonderful elements of life. It relates to the *positive focus principle* by forcing you to shift your focus on what you do want and do have, rather than on what you don't. The reality is that you have so much, but to enjoy it, you have to know how to notice it.

This doesn't mean that you should not strive for more, indeed you should, but whatever more you will get is a bonus, it's an additional luxury, not a necessity. If that luxury is a result of true effort, and even if you "just got lucky" on this occasion and it is not, then by all means enjoy it. However that is not really where happiness is. As I will state in the *Authentic Achievement* chapter, a focus on the future should only make up a small part of your day. The majority of happiness is to be found in the present, in utilizing what you do have right now.

The Power of Gratitude

The research relating to regular gratitude practice as a way to boost happiness and improve mental health is highly compelling. A classic study done by Robert Emmons and Mike McCullough randomly assigned their subjects to keep a daily diary for two weeks. One group wrote about what they were grateful for, another about their hassles and the third just wrote about life events. Joy, happiness and life satisfaction significantly and substantially increased in the gratitude group. Similar findings have been repeated many times.

If you can be genuinely grateful for all that you have, then you have nothing to lose when things don't go your way. Many leaders throughout history have spoken about the importance of gratitude. Gratitude is cultivated by making a conscious effort to actually appreciate and give thanks to the gifts or experiences you have had. It forces you to shift your focus and in order to think of, and appreciate, the positive aspects of your day, your world and your life.

It is also timeless as you can enjoy experiences of the past, a current experience and even an experience yet to happen. Even a negative aspect of your day could be viewed as positive if you examine it in an empowering way. You could, if you choose, even feel grateful for a difficult experience if you use it to learn and grow.

Gratitude practice can be incorporated into daily life quickly and effectively. Simply obtain a journal and each day answer "I am grateful for …" and then write down a minimum of three things that occurred that day for which you are grateful. With each experience, spend about 30-60 seconds reliving that experience as fully as possible. You can be grateful for anything, a sunrise, a type of food, a loved one, a fun time, having a particular object, your heart beat, your breath, your brain it does not matter. If you repeat yourself over time, that is fine; simply aim to enjoy a different aspect of that experience.

Giving

Gratitude is the practice of acknowledging and enjoying in new ways (thus avoiding habituation and training positive focus) the gifts in your life. However, since we are social creatures and designed to connect to others, the giving of a gift with another tends to create an even more unique experience and amplify positive emotion for the giver and receiver.

The power of giving has also been tested many times. A classic experiment (repeated many times) offered people a small amount of money to obtain a gift. One group was to purchase something for themselves whilst the other was to purchase a gift for someone else. Although both groups felt happier, the group that obtained a gift for another person showed much higher happiness scores. Additionally, gifts related to an experience (e.g. dinner, a show, a trip) tend to be more enjoyed than an object as they create more novel experiences and are easier to share and talk about with others.

I have a happiness challenge where I teach others to become happier and less stressed in just a couple minutes a day. However, participants are also encouraged to seek sponsorship for charity when doing the challenge because although learning how to be happier is great, raising money for others at the same time greatly amplifies the whole experience. The challenge is in my book, *Happiness Up Stress Down*.

Giving is extremely powerful for boosting mental health. The only caveat is that when you give, it should be because you want to give. If you are giving in hope of getting love or to please others, or because you feel obliged, the power of the experience will be greatly reduced. When you give, simply because you want to give, you are coming from a place of abundance which trains your mind into knowing you have more than enough and you can share it. Almost everything you have is a luxury anyway and small and thoughtful gifts are usually better than large ones as well.

Giving from a place of abundance is crucial. I know that several times in the past after suffering a large and often unfair financial setback, apart from promising myself to work to avoid it in the future, I have forced myself to give some money away to charity to remind me that I still have more than enough and the most meaningful and empowering thing we can do is help others. By giving, even when I feel hard done by, I am training myself out of scarcity and into abundance.

Abundance and Scarcity

Of course, being grateful and giving is all well and good, but it's still not fair that the Joneses have more, right? The whole idea of the Joneses is a consumerist creation to make you impulsive, self-centered and stupid. It is to lead you into feeling jealous, greedy and hard done by so you spend money you don't have on things you don't need because you now think you deserve it even though you may have actually done nothing to earn it. These entitlement beliefs run directly against the *Authentic Achievement Principle* to be revealed and are a recipe for unhappiness. No matter what you have, it will never be enough and you will never feel satisfied unless it is earned.

When it comes to perceiving life, people tend to fall into two distinct types of mindsets. One is abundance, with gratitude being its foundation, and the other is fear-based scarcity. Abundance promotes the belief that there are more than enough resources and opportunities for everyone to have an honest chance at creating health and happiness, whilst scarcity suggests a lack of opportunity and resources. Abundance parallels with pleasure seeking, positive focus and optimism whilst scarcity feeds off pain avoidance and pessimism. A scarcity focused mind can easily fall into anxiety and depression. An abundance focused mind is crucial for developing greater mental health.

The Heart of Abundance

At the heart of abundance must rest the belief that we have infinite resources. Not in the material but in the immaterial sense. In other words, we do not have infinite physical resources, but we do have infinite capability for resourcefulness. It is resourcefulness (gratitude is part of this), not resources that create abundance. Some people are gifted with millions of dollars and lose it all, whilst others start with nothing and accumulate vast fortunes. Several of the wealthiest companies in the world are based on technologies that did not exist a generation ago and were started in garages with virtually no start-up funds.

Even the greatest resource issue we face, the sustainability of the planet itself, could be solved. The technology required for abundant and sustainable living already exists. If everyone had a resourceful, innovative, abundance based mindset, there would be no environmental sustainability issue. Abundance is not about believing that we have the right and the luxury to be wasteful. Rather, it is about maximizing resources, seeking opportunities and creating new value through true effort. He or she who creates the most value, shall be the most mentally prosperous. This attitude is also most likely to lead to sustainable financial success as well. You are surrounded by opportunities for greater joy, accomplishment and happiness and that is something to be grateful for.

Principle Summary

Gratitude: Gratitude and giving are necessary practices and invaluable antidotes to greed, doubt, entitlement and other human pitfalls.

Gratitude is the key to enjoying and regularly re-sensitizing yourself to the wonders and of life and being giving creates larger feelings of pleasure than receiving. Avoid the entitlement mentality by acknowledging that we all live luxurious lives.

Fast-Action Techniques

1. Use the gratitude practice process revealed above and write down at least three things you are grateful for every day for two weeks. This is a very good exercise and something I previously did for 15 months straight.
2. Find three friends and/or three local causes or charities and offer each a small gift. Charities usually prefer money but books, clothes, appliances, or a helping hand may be appropriate. In regards to friends, make it a low cost and thoughtful gift. If you are able to create something, that is even better. It could be a cake, a poem, a piece of art or a fun night out! With at least one of them, do it anonymously.
3. When facing challenges, ask yourself abundance based questions. Regularly ask yourself "how could I add value and find opportunities to … utilize this failure (or success) for future (additional) success/ improve my work/ make someone else's life more enjoyable? And, so on. Brainstorm three new abundance based ideas a week.

Hypnotic Recording – The Gratitude and Abundance Attitude: For guided assistance in moving beyond the principles and techniques of this chapter, a guided brain re-training process to assist you in increasing life satisfaction and contentedness, being less attached to luxury items and developing a more abundant, curious and opportunity focused mindset is available now at - http://mentalhealthhypnosis.com/gratitudeandabundance

Meaning
Find meaning in life and a strong purpose in order to increase happiness and reduce suffering

A young therapist is about to meet his client. He has been dreading this moment all week. He knows the client is deeply depressed, possibly suicidal. He feels way out of his comfort zone. All those years of training have been leading up to a moment like this. Up until this point, he's tried just about everything to reach the client, to make a connection and nothing has worked.

Before she is to come in, he asks himself an important question. He ponders it for what feels an eternity, but must only be a couple of minutes. He is still unsure of the answer and without thinking he writes down the question and puts it aside leaving it unanswered. He works hard to mask his beating heart and shortness of breath and calls her in.

She enters the room. Her beauty is masked. Dark make-up and hair tightly pulled back with an expression of disdain. Staring him down, she moves to take a seat. She doesn't want to be there. She doesn't want to be anywhere. She is hard, and cold and fierce. She knows how this will go. She thinks: "What's this dumb kid going to try and sell me on today? That I should just get over it? Be nicer to people, call my family, and play a sport?" Starting to feel a deep sense of contempt, she takes a deep breath to speak when …

"Why haven't you ended your life?"

She is shocked, confused and taken aback.

He says it again, only more slowly, "why haven't you ended your life?"

She scans his face and is bewildered by what she sees. There is no malice or anger in his expression. There is no judgment, and yet he is firm. He is serious and unmoving, but also genuinely curious. She will not be able to escape it.

The pressure is building, cracks in the façade start to show. It just got raw, real and honest. Of course, she doesn't want to die. She wants to live but doesn't know how. Yet, in that moment, underneath the pain is a subtle surge of exhilaration. In her mind, she catches a foggy glimpse of a new path starting to unfurl.

He sits and waits patiently, caringly peering into her eyes. When she is ready, she will speak and through the flood of emotion, direction will be found. Over on the desk is a piece of paper. On it is the question he wrote. It was actually two questions.

What is her purpose? What is mine?

Visionless Wandering

Welcome to the age of neon enlightenment. All is not what it seems. Who are you and why are you here? Most people struggle to find a genuine answer to this question. They know what they think they want, according to what other people and flashy advertising have told them, but they don't really understand what they truly have to offer and what they are designed to contribute to the world. This is another one of my mental viruses that I refer to as Visionless Wandering.

Searching for the meaning of our lives is the most important task we can undertake. It is also the most fear inducing, as what we hold most sacred, our identity, is tied into the answer. Not knowing the answer is psychologically disturbing as we are designed to create meaning wherever we go. Many will try and avoid it, and a person may freeze when this topic is brought up, hoping that at some point the whole issue will just go away. If continually asked, a person may even become frustrated and angry towards anyone talking about the topic.

So many people are lost and directionless. They have no greater vision and struggle to deal with the pain and loneliness of modern life. **Even with so much information available, sorting through the negativity to find inspiring role-models and credible knowledge is challenging.** Wisdom seems harder to find now. The simple distinctions between right and wrong, good and evil, have been blurred through complication, confusion, artificial relationships and overstimulation.

There is a yearning for simplicity, a deep desire for real connections and true, meaningful direction. Creating a simple and positive purpose that is empowering and elegant is the greatest way to live and the smartest way to tackle any task. Some may say, "But, what if I commit to pursuing something and then I find out it's not what I really want?" The answer is, "That's still great!" Doing nothing important because you feel overwhelmed is much worse and you will still grow in a variety of ways through any meaningful pursuit. Furthermore, you can always change and adjust your purpose whenever you want to.

Perhaps it will help if I answer the greatest philosophical question we have. The question is: What is the meaning of life?

And, the answer is ...

Wait for it ...

Here it comes ...

Almost there ...

It's ...

I DON'T KNOW!

But ...

What if I said, **you're asking the wrong question?**

The question you should be asking is ...

What is the meaning of **MY LIFE?** Now, that is a question you can answer by developing your own unique purpose. Have you ever met someone who had lost their sense of purpose? Or, have you ever been in that position yourself? It's a horrible place to be. I would have to say without a doubt that one of the biggest reasons why so many people are so depressed these days is because they have no clear sense of purpose. Too many people are coasting along hoping that inspiration and meaning will find them.

Well, the truth is ...

You need to find it!

All inspiring people are inspiring because of their sense of purpose. Think about it now, who do you respect and admire and why do you respect and admire them? It's because in some way, you too believe in what they stand for. You can see, hear and feel what their purpose is. You experience it with them because that is the other secret about it. A true purpose must be bigger than yourself!

Happiness is always amplified when it is shared with others. Your purpose must not only make you happy, it must also be designed to serve others. Whether it's your family, friends, community or the greater world, your purpose must help others also find an empowering direction.

Here are three simple questions to answer now, but also reflect on often and return to on a regular basis. Write down (or say out loud if writing materials are not available) in as much detail as possible as many answers as you can to these three questions. Then commit to living by your answers.

1. For what would I like to be known?
2. How would I like to be described by others?
3. What must I start to **learn**, **be** and **do** from this moment on, in order to move me towards my greater purpose that will serve myself and others?

Acceptance and Transformation of Suffering

In life, you will suffer. Many events that you cannot control will harm you. Often those events are inside your own mind and body. It is something that must be accepted rather than fought. Through acceptance, meaning can be sought. Meaning comes by seeking lessons and direction from your own mindful self-observation.

As a general guide, anxiety is often related to a fear of failure. Anger is often because you feel something unfair has happened, and sadness comes from a lack of control. Often large and initially overpowering events will lead to sadness, whilst guilt and shame are usually related to the idea that you have done something wrong. In relation to all of these emotions, you do your best to right the wrongs if you can or make peace with what has occurred and seek to prevent additional pain in the future.

It is not always easy to connect to the deeper lessons and transform suffering. It requires patience and a kindness towards yourself and others. The lessons will not always be immediately obvious. When in doubt, turn to your values. They offer direction as you continue to seek meaning. (A structured values process is offered in the Valuable Living Chapter.) No matter how you feel, you can act in a way that compliments your values when unsure of what to do.

Finding your purpose, or if unsure at the time, acting purposefully in a manner that compliments your values is the ultimate elixir to the challenges of modern life. It is your guiding light through all the obstacles and the path to inspired and meaningful living that serves your needs and those of others as well. Whatever fear you may have, can be overcome if you have a big enough reason to beat it. A compelling purpose allows you to consistently access and act on that reason.

Spirituality and Religion

To seek a greater spiritual understanding of the purpose of life is a challenging but often worthwhile process. Asking deeper questions and connecting to the nature of things can be very beneficial as long as it is done from a perspective of curiosity, humility and non-judgement. Being spiritual is often a part of but not considered the same as being religious. One can be spiritual without being religious.

Much research has shown that religious people tend to be happier than the non-religious. I believe the two core factors that being religious usually brings for people is socialization (being part of a group and connecting with others) and life direction. However it is also understandable that many people are weary of religion. Religious wars, corruption, molestation and other ills are realities that have been related to religion.

The issue is that a religion is still operated by humans, who are naturally flawed and judgemental. If you do wish to follow a religion, it is important to stay focused on the positive principles and be aware of the character of the people operating it. Never follow what a "leader" says without question and consideration of the greater impacts of an act. Whether religious or not, seek spiritual guidance from multiple people and choose your own path.

Principle Summary

Meaning: Find meaning in life and a strong purpose in order to increase happiness and reduce suffering.

Consider what you must continue to learn, be and do to find meaning (especially through difficult times) and create a strong purpose that will develop yourself and serves others. Observational acceptance of inevitable periods of suffering will lead to positive and transformative learning experiences.

Fast-Action Techniques

1. Purpose comes in two forms, immediate and grand. Practice asking "what is the purpose of this?" in relation to short term activities as well. What you will be doing is setting an intention, which tends to lead to better and more enjoyable outcomes. Asking what is the purpose of my gym session, or this meeting, or this meal etc. leads to being more focused on creating the actual outcome you want.
2. If you have not already, set aside some time this week to go through the three purpose questions offered earlier in the chapter more deeply. Aim to refine your answers and take a longer term view this time. Imagine it is many years from now and you are towards the end of your life and then answer those three questions from that perspective looking back to what you must change now. Then imagine implementing those answers into your life and envision three positive future events to occur because you will make those changes.
3. Review three painful events from your past. What meaning and lessons have you taken from them and what are you still

learning? How will you become stronger in the future because you have gotten through those experiences? Also consider how you could share your learnings with others to help them be stronger too.

Hypnotic Recording – Valuable and Meaningful Living: For guided assistance in moving beyond the principles and techniques of this chapter, a guided brain re-training process to assist you in living in accordance with your deepest values and with greater purpose and meaning so you can find fulfilment and the lessons required to overcome the most difficult life experiences is at - http://mentalhealthhypnosis.com/valuesandmeaning

Part 4: The Principles of Life Mastery

Authentic Achievement
Access the ultimate attitude and practice for superior mental health and creative accomplishment

There is a trap door in your mind. It is like the elephant in the room problem only in this instance, not only do you want the elephant gone, you are the one that invited the elephant in the beginning. Many times in the past the trap door has swung open and you, along with your elephant, have fallen through it. Do not feel I am singling you out. We've all done it. We've all been sat on by our own elephants. Trapped and suffocating under the weight of what we brought with us.

As simple as it is, many people will never overcome the mental trap door problem. They will continually be crushed by the elephant they are trying to get rid of and unknowingly invited. The whole problem rests on one simple proposition. It is a classic "if/then" statement.

It goes like this "If I achieve X, then I will be happy." Or, another way it may be framed is "because I haven't achieved X, I can't be happy." Whatever your "X" is, it is also your elephant. You cannot overcome your elephant. Even if you achieve X, the elephant will simply return even larger than before.

What you have done is you have made your happiness determinant on your success. You have given over your power to the idea of success. This leads to two massive problems. The first is you can't control every aspect of success. Life is often unfair and brutal. Many events out of your control will continually test you and interfere with your success.

The second problem is there is always a greater "X." You can never really win. The elephant will just get bigger! There is always another level of success to aspire towards and so one of only two things can ever occur. The first is you do not achieve your X, and therefore spend your whole life being miserable. Or, you do achieve X, feel good for a little while (until habituation occurs), and then start the new cycle, miserably seeking the bigger X.

Whether you succeed or not, you are driven by pain. The feeling of success never stays. Even when you win, you lose! The alternative is "If I am happy, then I will be successful." Actually it should be "If I am happy, then I am successful," however we will go with the first phrase (and make a slight addition to it) because we are focusing on achievement. "If you are happy, then you will be *more* successful."

Achievement

Having a sense of achievement is extremely important to our happiness and mental health. Even the simplest things, and the activities you hate, once completed give us an emotional boost and a sense of achievement. Brushing teeth and washing dishes for example are activities people rarely find enjoyable, however there is always an emotional boost (even if only mild) when finished.

When someone is depressed, they tend to stop doing things and start losing those emotional boosts. Types of activities to be done are ones that increase pleasure. Those activities are good, and they are a great initial method for improving mood. They are not as important as activities that also offer a sense of achievement. Passive pleasure, focused activities such as reading, looking at pictures, watching a video, listening to music etc., are not as powerful as their active counterparts – writing, taking pictures, filming, playing music.

Passive pleasures are easier, and thus if really feeling low, a great place to begin in order to build emotional momentum. However once enough momentum has been gathered, the idea is to move onto an active pleasure that is also going to offer a much higher sense of achievement.

Seduced by Undeserving Progression

Having a sense of progression is psychologically important to us. It is ingrained in our natural (e.g. physical growth) and cultural (e.g. schooling) learning cycles. As we grow and develop, there is an expectation of an increase in skill. However, this expectation often seduces people to take short cuts, cheat or simply to assume the skill will be satisfactorily learnt without the required effort.

Many adult (and child) learning courses fall into this trap. The assumption is made that attendance is enough for competence, but without active application of the material through testing, abilities may fall much shorter in reality than expected. Since no testing took place, those learning gaps will be invisible and cannot be fixed.

Being social creatures, we also tend to compare ourselves to others. Since we have a (often inaccurate) bias towards noticing pain, we often see others in a way that highlights their strengths and their successes over ours. By feeling less worthy than the other person, we feel driven to quickly progress towards their level or even beyond it.

There are three issues with this. The first is related to causal perceptions. The reason they may "have" or "be" more than you is because of one or a combination of the following: luck, additional help, greater dedication or more talent. In terms of talent, what we tend to do and should not, is unfairly compare our limitations against another person's strengths. We also rarely consider their limitations in relation to our strengths. We look for where they are better but tend to ignore the other areas where we may be better.

The second is misperception. You may be sucked into the fantasy projection. Today's world allows people to appear much more talented and affluent than they actually are. People show what they want to show and hide what they can hide. A new home, nice car, great suit, job title, awards won, and relationship status are not necessarily a true reflection of how someone is travelling. For example, having the latest items at the cost of being in extreme debt is something that is very common today and not a choice I would recommend. The Global Financial Crisis of 2008 was based on this very problem.

Third and most important, will it actually make you happy? Achieving as much as your friend or colleague at X, or having what they have and more, will it actually make you happy? No!

Your success (if you can call it that) is being driven by pain avoidance rather than actual pleasure seeking which means the rewards for your success are mostly external. Deep inside yourself, you know most of these things don't matter very much to you and now in order to protect your supposed advantage, you will have to keep going to the next level.

The bigger house, the promotion, all the things you think you are supposed to care about, and what advertising in a consumerist society pushes on you isn't really for you, it's for them. Most of the things you achieve become more and more meaningless. Every time you win, you lose! So what's the answer?

Authentic Achievement

Happiness breeds success much more than success breeds happiness. This has been proven countless times in the literature. Happiness tends to lead to optimism (the biggest predictor of life success) and greater productivity in terms of efficiency, creativity and motivation. Is it not easier to motivate yourself to do something you actually want to do and naturally enjoy? Positive emotion creates more energy, more drive and more success.

The catch is you have to commit to pursuing what makes you truly happy. Doesn't sound like much of a problem, but for many it really is. When you fail at things you really care about, the hurt is much deeper. When you go against the norms of a consumerist society or the advice of influential people in your life, it's scary as you don't want to look foolish or be seen as a disappointment. When you discover that real progression is not always positive and linear, it's extremely frustrating. In those times, it would be wise to review and solidify the positive focus, optimism, self-image and mindful acceptance principles of this book.

However, nothing, and I do mean nothing, feels as good as achieving something you truly care about. The achievement must be earned; it can't be given to you. A diploma without true testing is just a piece of paper. Happiness is based on effort and achievement, not external signs of success. A study was done many years ago that compared two very happy groups of people. Both believed they had earned their success. One group was up to eight times wealthier than the other group and yet both groups were equally happy.

It also does not matter what level you are starting from or where you end up, as long as you are continually working to improve. You are seeking progression in its truest form, without cheating or unfair comparison. When working on improving yourself, it is always better to primarily focus on level of effort as opposed to success. Too many things, often out of your control can unfairly diminish your success on any given day. However, if you still did your best despite those challenges, than you are still successful and will become more successful in terms of results over time too.

Everyday Happiness

Throughout this book I have spoken about the importance of mindfulness. Mindfulness is about connecting to and enjoying the present. You must follow the same principle in terms of achievement and happiness. The majority of your day needs to be focused on the small victories you achieved during that day. It is in those small moments of insight and creative progression that most of the happiness lies.

That is not to say that you shouldn't dream about and plan for future success. You absolutely should! However, being future focused (and enjoying the experience) should only make up a relatively small portion of your day, perhaps spending some time at the start and end of each day (or maybe the week) to connect to and adjust your future goals and ambitions. What is most important is to enjoy the process rather than the result. The aim is to be happy, and therefore successful.

Start Slow and Don't Ignore your Responsibilities

Making sudden and drastic life changes in the pursuit of greater authentic achievement is not advisable. We all have responsibilities and they should always be respected. It can also be a difficult process and gradual change is much easier to cope with than sudden change. My recommendation is to either find or work to enhance a current creative pursuit. Build up to scheduling in more creative pursuits over time. I truly believe we are happiest when we are creating, when working on an active pleasure as opposed to experiencing passive one.

To assist you with this, I will add a Creativity Boosting Process from "Destiny Defining Decisions," my book on entrepreneurship. Entrepreneurship in many ways is one of the greatest ways to achieve authentic living, but it is not for everyone and also a very difficult and risky journey. If you wish to find out more, a link is provided in the personal bibliography.

Achieving when Mood is Very Low

Unfortunately, during difficult or depressive times we can fall into a difficult place in our learning cycle. It can feel like we have gone backwards and even the simplest tasks can feel very challenging. The same principles apply. You must remain as active as you can. Utilize your pure pleasures if needed and re-develop your skills by committing to achieve simple tasks and day by day build up from there. Effort is more important than overall success. Seek the lessons and as your mood improves, your skills will leap ahead towards where they should be as well.

Principle Summary

Authentic Achievement: Access the ultimate attitude and practice for superior mental health and creative accomplishment.

Achieving is crucial to happiness but works only when it is in relation to what you truly care about. The greatest satisfaction comes when you have had to stretch yourself in terms of effort and creativity and when you believe that you have really earned the reward.

Fast-Action Techniques

1. With creativity boosting it is important to realize that the principles you learn in one field, if intelligently applied, relate the

enhancement and originality of who you become in other fields. Here is a simple 5-step step checklist process to help you discover and develop your creativity boosting options.

1) Create a list of all the creative activities you find enjoyable. If you struggle to create a list of at least 10, do an internet search of lists of creative activities related to Music, Art, Design, Writing, Sports, Crafts, Computing, Engineering, Hobbies, Drama, Dance and anything else you can think of, and tick off ones of interest.
2) Review your past and childhood. List all the activities you used to enjoy in the past. Go right back into your childhood and explore old creative works if you still have them.
3) Consider your current and previous interests and ask yourself how much do you enjoy these activities and why.
4) Create a list of online sites about creativity and local places in your area that could trigger ideas. Consider museums, festivals, shows, open nights, particular interest groups, and so on. Also consider talking to creative friends and generating ideas from them and schedule visits to such places.
5) Decide on a new creative pursuit, or develop enhancements to an existing creative pursuit and answer: How can I apply in three new ways the skills developed from this creative pursuit to improve my daily life and/or in relation to a specific project? For example: If you decide to take acting classes, how could you use what you learn to interact better with clients, control emotions, or improve preparation for certain career transitions and roles? If exploring art, consider such things as: how could I improve the design of my reports, improve my work or home environment and add more color, flair, and originality to my wardrobe?

2. Focus on effort rather than success and respect your learning cycles. You will sometimes go backwards and will need to

exercise patience. Test yourself regularly and seek honest progression. Rate yourself on a scale of 1-10 each day for a week based on your creative efforts rather than successes.
3. Keep your focus in the present for most of the day. You may want to spend 10 minutes at the start and/or end of each day focusing and enjoying a wonderful potential future based on your current creative efforts, but sustainable happiness must be found in the present. Aim to appreciate and enjoy both the struggles and victories of your daily challenges.

Hypnotic Recording – Creativity and Achievement: For guided assistance in moving beyond the principles and techniques of this chapter, a guided brain re-training process to assist you on boosting creative power and increasing authentic daily happiness and achievement skills is available at the following link - http://mentalhealthhypnosis.com/creativityandachievement

Easy Goal Setting and Accountability
This is the simplest and easiest goal setting process you will ever come across so you can stop procrastinating and start succeeding

The clock continues to tick! Each reverberation of sound acts as a tiny dagger to the heart. She sits there paralyzed. There is so much inside, so much to offer, but where does she start? A few doors down he is feeling the exact same way, and so are countless others. They all hide behind distractions and excuses and the dream continues to slip away. One could have been a novelist, another a painter, one an engineer, and another a dancer. A week passes, a month, a year and even decades go by. Still the clock ticks, their hearts bleed and they remain still.

If only they just started, if they just made the first goals really small and built from there rather than fixating on the overall size of the aspiration. If only they took that step and told other supportive people of their authentic ambition rather than hiding in the shadows. If only ... However, it is not too late! As long as a heart still beats, new creation is possible.

To be successful, you must set goals. When I say success, I am referring not just to your work, but to all aspects of your life. In the past, I have developed deep and detailed goal setting processes and it's possible to write an entire book on goal setting alone, but to dive into a highly detailed goal setting process now would be overwhelming and unnecessary.

This is a book of mental health developing principles. It is better to give you a process that is as streamlined as possible, so you can start now! One secret to success is to make your initial goals in any area as easy as possible so you can build momentum. Success breeds success. My goal is for you to begin by setting 1-2 small and easy goals for yourself by the end of this section.

You can get on the right track now with a simple 3-step goal setting process. Before I reveal it, the question that needs to be answered is: Why is goal setting important? If you want to succeed at something, you must set a goal to do it. Think about it; just about everything you do in a day is achieved because you set a goal to do it. Brushing your teeth is a goal, eating lunch is a goal and getting to work on time is a goal.

The question is not do you set goals, the question is do you set empowering goals? How do you set empowering goals? By actually sitting down and asking yourself what is it that you really want in your life. It may help to break up your life into different categories so you have a more complete picture of your life.

You could break up your life into these basic categories.

Health

Finances

Career

Passions/Hobbies

Intimate Relationships

Family Relationships

Relationships Other

Then choose just one category to begin with. Let's take Passions/Hobbies.

Let's say you are an artist and your busy life is interfering with your ability to get your art project done. Here is how you could get your project done.

1. **Estimate how long you actually think it would take to complete the project.** If you are new to structured goal setting, then to be safe, add an extra 30-50% to the estimated timeframe. Things almost always get in the way and it can be discouraging at first. If you are new to the process, considerably overestimate how long it will take. If you are wrong about your estimate and you get it done sooner, great, you can create a more accurate estimate for the next project.
2. **Details, details, details.** Be very specific about how and when you will do everything related to the goal. These are called

sub-goals. The more specific you are, the more likely you are to follow through on the goal process each time. For example, it could look something like this:
   a. Tomorrow at 7am, I will get up and spend half an hour at the most examining my art supplies and taking inventory. In my lunch break at 12:30, I'll go to the art store and purchase everything I need for the project.
   b. Tonight, immediately after dinner, I will clear my art study and prepare all materials. Then my regular procedure will be this.
   c. Mon, Wed, Fri: Each session is a minimum of 1 hour up to a maximum of 2 hours. The aim will be about 1.5 hours. Each session will begin between 9 and 9:20pm and I must work on the project for at least one full hour regardless of how I am feeling.
   d. I will set aside 10 minutes in the beginning for warm up creativity exercises and 10 minutes at the end for clean-up and preparation for the next session.
3. **Review Progress** – Each week until the goal is completed, spend the time needed to review progress and readjust the estimated time of completion. For example, every Sunday night immediately after dinner, I will spend 10-20 minutes reviewing progress and setting expectations for the following week. As a highly recommended bonus, promise yourself a reward each week if you complete what you set out to do. There you go, a very simple three-step goal setting process that you can begin immediately.

Goal Setting Exercise

Choose a goal and follow the process just outlined. First, choose a category to focus on. Then follow the basic process explained.

   1. Create a goal completion time-frame estimate.
   2. Make your sub-goals as detailed and specific as possible and commit to them.
   3. Review Progress by setting aside a particular time each week to do so.

I told you it was simple. However, setting a goal is not the same as committing to complete a goal. An intelligent goal setter will also set up accountability measures. To assist you here, I've outlined my 4 Ps of accountability.

4 Ps of A-level Accountability

Below are the 4 Ps of accountability and some quick strategies on how to best incorporate each of the principles. Be aware that they are in ascending level of power. In other words, the 4th P is the highest level of accountability, but all four are beneficial and work best when all utilized together.

The 4 Ps are:

- **Personal accountability**
- **Partner accountability**
- **Party accountability**
- **Public accountability**

The first person you have to be accountable to is "you." As part of this stage you are to get clear on your compelling reasons for pursuing the goal and write out a list of the benefits of obtaining the goal and consequences of not obtaining it. Then narrow the list to the top five most emotionally intense benefits and consequences.

Place the list in a highly visible place or in multiple places and review frequently.

To enhance personal accountability, consider crafting a mission statement, creating a scrapbook with relevant images, journaling on your commitment, and developing a set of beliefs, rules, and expectations that you verbally declare to follow through on a regular basis. Put as many positive reminders of the goal in your environment as possible.

The next level up is becoming accountable to a "partner." Being vulnerable and declaring your goals in front of another person is difficult.

What you want at this level is someone who is supportive, trustworthy, positive, but also firm. Your partner **CAN NOT** be an "it's okay" kind of person. You have to hate the idea of disappointing them, as they will not be accepting of any run-of-the-mill excuses.

Checking in on a regular basis, preferably daily, is best and to enhance the process, making friendly bets should be incorporated. The bet should offer a nice reward if you succeed and a reasonably annoying and irritating consequence if you do not. For example, if you are successful, your partner takes you out to your favourite restaurant, but if you fail you have to wash their car every week for a month.

The next level is to be accountable to a "party." Having not just one person but a group of people you are committed to will add support and usually increase compliance. Especially if you are in the right kind of group who all share similar beliefs, attitudes and are determined to succeed. Everything you do with a partner you can also do with a group, but now you are committed to more people.

The highest level of accountability is "public." This is where you do everything you can to tell everyone about your goal. Everyone you meet should know about it. It should be revealed across websites and social media channels, and questions from whomever must be encouraged and welcomed. You should brand yourself with your goal, perhaps making T-shirts and other paraphernalia related to it. At this level, it may even become a cause.

You may notice that this is what many celebrities will do if they have really struggled with a certain goal, usually weight loss. They will declare it publicly through the media and advertising. With so many people now aware of the goal, the potential pain and embarrassment for not succeeding is very high, but also the potential support and pleasure for succeeding is magnified many times over. Another example of accountability at this level is entering competitions or starting goal-related groups. When you go public, you have the opportunity to be a role-model and make a real positive social impact.

Success at this level is guaranteed to increase self-esteem, confidence, and pride. Even if only a few people learn of and actively support your efforts, your frequent public declarations show just how serious and committed you are. Those are the 4 Ps. Ideally, you want to cater to all four levels. Consider a goal you currently have and work through this process.

Principle Summary

Easy Goal Setting and Accountability: This is the simplest and easiest goal setting process you will ever come across so you can stop procrastinating and start succeeding.

The more specific and detailed you make your goal, the easier it is follow. Writing it down and setting up accountability measures will dramatically increase chances of success.

Fast-Action Techniques

1. Write down three goals you would like to achieve over the next year. Then narrow it down to just one, whichever is most authentically important to you at this time of your life. Write it down three times (attach related images as well if you like) and place each piece of paper in three different and highly visible places. Then write a long list of benefits of achieving the goal and consequences of not obtaining it.
2. Do the three-step goal set process. Estimate total length of time required for completion, write out a detailed plan of actions and a scheduled weekly review time to adjust sub-goals and finish date as you progress. Finally, reward yourself at the end of each weekly review.
3. Set up your accountability measures and partners. You can start simply with only a few measures (as long as it will keep you committed), but aim to continually build your accountability measures over time. Only start an additional major goal after you have set up what you need and are confident of maintaining the first. Then repeat all above steps again for the next goal and so on.

Easy Goal Setting and Accountability

Hypnotic Recording – Fast Goal Setting and Accountability Made Easy: For guided assistance in moving beyond the principles and techniques of this chapter, a guided brain re-training process to assist you in increasing commitment to the development and completion of inspiring and authentic goals and becoming happily accountable to them is available now at this link - http://mentalhealthhypnosis.com/goalsandaccountability

Valuable Living
Undertake simple values clarification in order to know how to consistently live your best life

If I suddenly dropped you in the middle of a foreign place, what would be the first thing you would do? I assume you would scan your environment in order to determine how you should behave (how cautious should you be) and then seek signs in order to establish direction. You meet friendly locals, but none of them know where you come from, so they can only offer their best suggestions for what you should do.

Following their advice should lead you to safety but won't get you back home. Unless you discover the signs that can lead you home, you will remain trapped in this foreign place. Although over time, you may learn to adjust, it never feels quite right because you never chose to live there. Their beliefs, behavior and lifestyle are just too different from yours, and so you will always be searching for a way home.

A value is a core principle that is also attached to a feeling and a standard of behavior that is personally important to you. Ideally, the best values are the ones you totally believe in, feel deeply and act on frequently. Unfortunately, many people do not live by their highest values. This is either because of unawareness, short term pain avoidance or lack of discipline in implementation. Surprisingly, the biggest reason why people do not live by their highest values is simply because they do not know what they are.

Since it is survival and not happiness that is our primary instinctual priority, our own core values are not automatically available to us. In fact, what most people think are their values (if they think about them at all), is usually the result of what has been conditioned into them by external influences. Through our attempts to avoid pain and seek pleasure and in order to find stability and progress, we absorb and follow the values of those with the most influence over us. Primarily, they will be the values of your parents, but also that of other role-models, friends, community standards and the greater social status quo.

It is highly likely that your adopted values have served their primary purpose which is to keep you safe from harm. However, pain avoidance based living will not increase your happiness or strengthen your mental health. Values act as the director in life. How you are being directed is going to determine the quality of the experiences you have on set. The set is your life! Valued direction will guide you like a compass to take certain paths and avoid others. Knowing this, is it not crucial that you receive the right direction?

What if the director is indecisive, easily confused or makes conflicting choices? What if he or she frequently feels overwhelmed by choice or bored because of a perceived lack of options? What if your director cannot actually read or even find a compass?

There are four stages when it comes to values driven living.

- Extract
- Align
- Express
- Adjust

First you must *extract* your own core values. Your intention is to find what you need to raise your standards of behavior. Then you *align* them in their proper sequence so they are easy to pursue. Following this you *express* them by behaving in accordance with the chosen values and finally you *adjust* any of the previous three areas accordingly based on the feedback you receive.

Values Extraction

Extracting core values is actually quite a simple process. All that is required is to ask yourself two simple questions. The first is "What do I want in life?" For example, you may say a big house, more money, deeper friendships, family, a new car, a better job and so on. At this point it is important to realize that these are not values but goals. Goals are the potential tangible results of a value being met. None of the above are core principles attached to feelings and a standard of behavior. To extract the actual value, a second question is asked.

The second question is "What would having this lead me to feel?" Therefore, if I asked you what would having a big house lead you to feel and you said "secure," security is a value. In addition you might reveal that a large house would allow you to have a large group of your friends over. When I ask what emotion would that lead you to feel you may say "fun", or "love." Fun and love are values. If you wanted money and I asked why, you may respond, "So, I can be free to do what I want." Freedom is a value.

A different person may want more money for a different reason. They may say they want money so that if anything happens to their family, they would have enough to care for their loved ones, in that case security would be the value. Someone else may say I want the money so I can "take it easy and just relax." In that case, comfort would be the value. You may want money to feel all three of those values, but one in particular will be guiding your decisions more than the others.

It is also important to realize that unlike a goal, values cannot be achieved. You cannot achieve love. You are either being more or less loving at any moment. You cannot achieve security. You are either feeling more or less secure at any moment. This is the same with fun, freedom, and comfort. Several people may want the same thing, but they may all want it for different emotional reasons.

Values Alignment

Once your values have been extracted, the next step is alignment. Alignment relates to ranking your values in the correct order to avoid inner conflict. For example, if "freedom" is your highest value, but "security" is your second highest, you are likely to become indecisive. Here, you will need to examine what you truly want and either move one of those values further down the list or possibly remove one altogether. In most cases in an example like this, the value that is moved or dropped is "security."

The first reason why this is likely is because "freedom" is actually ranking higher. The second reason is "security" is usually defined in a way that is pain avoidance based, and if you truly want to live your best life, you should have an overall focus on seeking pleasure. Thirdly, depending on the perspective you take (focusing on what you do want as opposed to what you do not, e.g. "less fat" or "more trim", "less stressed" or "more relaxed" – See Positive Focus Principle), by focusing on becoming truly free, this may allow you to feel even more secure. If you become less attached to what you think you need to make you secure and instead aim for greater freedom, you may find an even deeper sense of security within that freedom.

Values Expression and Adjustment

Once you have found and aligned your values, the next step is expression. Your aim is to make them real by utilizing them in your daily life. Your values are there to guide and flavor your mentally healthy lifestyle. In terms of guiding your life, the question to ask is "What tasks will I choose to do today that will best compliment my values?" In relation to flavoring your life, ask "What value/s will I express in order to enhance my experience of this task?" The first question is best asked at the beginning of each day and the second question is to be kept in mind, answered and acted upon frequently throughout the day.

The final step is adjustment. As you progress, you may need to change your values, re-align the order and sequence or learn how to express them more effectively in order to find the right life balance. This is not a process that is to be done once and never repeated or adjusted.

Developing Mental Health Guidelines: Extracting and Aligning Your Values

Exercise 1 - Excavation: What do you want in life? Spend 5-10 minutes writing down your answers to this question. For example, is it more money, better or more friends, increased health, new experiences and so on? Write down everything and anything you can think of that you would want. To assist you, also consider what you want in relation to categories of life. Consider what you want in relation to health, finances, personal growth, spirituality, hobbies, career, relationships, fun and experiences.

Once you have a large list, ask yourself in relation to each item "What would having this lead me to feel?" This question will get to the value. You may have to ask it more than once per item to get you to the deeper value. You will also notice certain patterns and repetitive themes emerge. For additional prompting, below is an incomplete personal values list.

Personal Values List

- Love
- Courage
- Security
- Abundance
- Prosperity
- Passion
- Compassion
- Intelligence
- Health/Vitality
- Confidence/Self-assuredness
- Flexibility/Adaptability
- Cheerfulness
- Curiosity
- Fun
- Joy
- Adventure
- Freedom
- Creativity
- Gratitude
- Honour
- Integrity
- Contribution
- Harmony

- Comfort
- Determination
- Optimism
- Discipline
- Loyalty
- Commitment
- Perseverance

Other: Any extra values defined in your own words:

_____
_____
_____
_____
_____

Exercise 2 – Alignment: Examine your values list and circle between 5-10 values that you know would lead to greater confidence, happiness and fulfillment.

Then rank them in order of preference and create a final list of no more than 3-5 values. Be careful not to place conflicting values near each other on the hierarchy. You can rank them intuitively or if uncertain, ask yourself this question: When I think of how I must live my life (in order to be authentic and healthy), am I guided more by _____ or _____?

E.g. When I think of how I must live my life (in order to be authentic and healthy), am I guided more by Courage or Freedom?

Answer: Courage. Then ask the same question with Courage and another of your top 10 values.

When I think of how I must live my life (in order to be authentic and healthy), am I guided more by Courage or Health?

Answer: Health.

Then you would continue comparing Courage with the other values. After finishing with Courage, you would compare another value like Freedom with each of the other values. If you select the values you think will be highest to compare with the others each time, you should be able to finish this process quite quickly.

Assuming that there are only three values to compare, I will complete this example. Although, this last comparison is not mathematically necessary.

When I think of how I must live my life (in order to be authentic and healthy), am I guided more by Health or Freedom?

Answer: Health.

So in this example:

1. Health
2. Courage
3. Freedom

If at any point you feel you begin to contradict yourself during this process, rank the contradictions intuitively.

MY FINAL VALUES RANKINGS

1. _____
2. _____
3. _____
4. _____
5. _____
6. _____
7. _____
8. _____
9. _____
10. _____

Exercise 3 – Expression: Now your goal is to live your values. The first question in order to do this is the daily question, "What tasks will I choose to do today that will best compliment my values?" The second question to be asked frequently is "What value/s will I express in order to enhance my experience of this task?" In the beginning, write down your answers to these questions each time they are asked and the results based on their implementation.

Exercise 4 – Adjustment: You can be too expressive or not expressive enough. For one week minimum, monitor the effects of your value based actions (based on how you feel, how others respond and how successful you are in relation to tasks) and evaluate how you feel overall at the end of each day in order to see if your values feel like they are in the right order. Simply journal about your experience. Make adjustments as necessary. Experiment with changing the order of your values and intensity and frequency of expression until you get the balance right.

Living by Your Values

Living by your values will develop your ability to understand yourself, leading to more confident and enjoyable living. In some ways values add to the "behavior is king" principle in conjunction with knowing what is most important to you. You can "act now" and set goals based on what your values are even if you do not feel or believe that you can. Being authentic is a major key to healthy and happy living and knowing and acting on your values allows you to do this.

Principle Summary

Valuable Living: Undertake simple values clarification in order to know how to consistently live your best life.

Discovering and living by your values will give you the greatest sense of freedom and meaningful direction. They are the best signposts for knowing what to do and how to act when facing difficult and uncertain choices.

Fast-Action Techniques

1. Complete the values process as described in this chapter and organize your top 3-5 values and answer the questions on how you will implement them.
2. Place your values in a highly visible place, so you can reflect on them often. Mine are written on a large piece of cardboard posted on the back of my home office door. Also consider

adding empowering images, quotes, poems, etc. that are reflective of your values.
3. To engrain your values, for at least 2-3 weeks, spend a few minutes each day reading them and describe how you will act in accordance with your values across a few different expected situations during the day. Be kind to yourself as well. You will never be perfect at this, values are signposts to keep turning to whenever we get off track and if after a period of time they don't seem to be feeling right for you, review your values and change them.

Hypnotic Recording – Valuable and Meaningful Living: For guided assistance in moving beyond the principles and techniques of this chapter, a guided brain re-training process to assist you in living in accordance with your deepest values and with greater purpose and meaning so you can find fulfilment and the lessons required to overcome the most difficult life experiences is at - http://mentalhealthhypnosis.com/valuesandmeaning

Peak Performance
Demonstrate positive discipline and high self-confidence by regularly triggering and intensifying the right emotion on command

Is emotion important? If "the law" is that we can only be judged by our "behavior" and the direction of our behavior is generally influenced by our focus (relating to thoughts, beliefs and expectations), is there ever a time when emotion supersedes the importance of the other two? Yes, there is! To best illustrate when emotion becomes most important, we need to go back to the Olympic 100 metre final.

Of course, once the starting gun fires, behavior determines victory. However, the race in many ways is mostly won before the gun fires. Every athlete should also have a belief that they are going to win, but if the belief is to have any real impact, it must be attached to the right emotion. Unlike most of our usual tasks, where empowering beliefs and emotions can catch up once we start behaving the right way, when it comes to a performance where first impressions are crucial or where every microsecond counts, before you begin, you must believe you will be successful and that belief will only have power if attached to the right feeling.

The "right feeling" will be different for every athlete. One will start to "aggressively pump" themselves up, listening to hard and angry metal music. Another will seek a feeling of deep serenity. Another may connect to a feeling of family love, whilst the next athlete taps into the excitement of the crowd. One may seek deep personal inspiration and another aims for precise calm neutrality.

Emotional priming

What each athlete is doing is getting into the right emotional state (or priming) for the upcoming task. Through trial and error and practice, each has come to realize that particular emotions are more useful than others for the task at hand. Once they have discovered what emotion or set of emotions are best, then they have to find ways to trigger them at the right time.

To be at your best, two critical questions must be answered. What emotions do you want to feel and how do you create different emotions? The emotions you want to feel depend on the task that you are doing. For the best performance, you want to create the appropriate emotion in yourself before you begin and re-fire it at key points during the task until it is completed.

The right emotion for the task can only be selected by you. Here is how you figure it out. When you are about to perform a task, think of a time in the past when you completed the same or a similar task in a way where you felt highly positive, productive and motivated. In psychology, this is called a "flow" state. In sport, it is often referred to being in the "zone." It develops from the synchronization of emotion and focus.

Whatever you were feeling at the time is what you need to produce in yourself again now in order to be as effective as you can be in doing the task. For example, let's say you are going to write a report. The kind of report you want to write will determine the kind of emotions you need to generate in order to have the most effective outcome.

If it's a technical report, filled with lots of scientific and detailed material, then the kind of emotion you may generate is one that encourages you to feel laser-focused, sharp, detail-orientated, critical and analytical. All you need to know is the descriptive words of what you want to feel. You won't need to know the name of the actual emotion/s.

In the previous example, the corresponding emotions may be a mixture of determination/discipline/commitment/fastidiousness. As I said, knowing the names of the specific emotions is not that important. All you need to be aware of are the words that support what you feel.

What if the report was not supposed to be technical, but more of an initial idea generator? Then you would need to access a different set of feelings. Here you may want to be more open, creative, flowing, abundant, and expansive. Maybe you need to start off as open, creative and expansive and as you go through it and begin to edit it, generate more analytical, critical and detail-orientated feelings.

Maybe your report is supposed to be exciting. Or, maybe it's not a report. Maybe you're about to write and give a speech! Then in this case perhaps you need to generate feelings of fun, joy, excitement, wonder, possibility, power, motivation. So how do you create the right motivational feelings you need for the task at hand? By manipulating your body and mind in a way that will encourage you to feel those emotions. It's like following a recipe and, fortunately, it's pretty easy to do.

One way is simply to imagine a time when you felt the way you want to be feeling. You might want to close your eyes if you like and really bring back that memory and immerse yourself in it. As you do that, bring your awareness to the way you were using your body and the kind of thoughts you were having.

You will then start to feel those same emotions again, your body will naturally change, and you will have access to thoughts that complement those feelings.

That's it! Now begin your task feeling active, engaged and motivated.

If you can't think of a previous time it still is not a problem. Your body knows how to create the emotions you want it to create, even if you can't think of a time when you felt it. Simply manipulate your body piece by piece in a way that you think would create the emotion/s you want to feel and you will create them.

Let's say you want to feel confident and determined (C&D). Right now sit or stand as someone who is C&D. Breathe the way a C&D person would breathe. Have the same facial expression as someone who is C&D would have.

Feel C&D yet? Or, do you need more prompts? Put your shoulders and chest in a C&D position. Now think the way a C&D person would think. Believe what a C&D person would believe and feel the way a C&D person would feel.

Advanced Emotional Priming – Adding the Full Power of Your Mind

Most professional athletes practice types of performance enhancing visualization. Many studies have shown how performance improves almost to the same level for those who vividly imagine exceptional performance as for those who actually spent the same amount of time physically practicing.

The secret is knowing how to use the full power of your imagination. I'm going to reveal a process for creating "mind movies" where you imagine your best-self performing at your peak with full experiential power. You work to see, hear, feel, smell, taste, and positively focus on being at your best across a range of different experiences.

You may need to read this exercise a few times before doing it. This exercise is the closest thing to hypnosis in this book because, like hypnosis, it requires deep focus and it works on triggering and enhancing key thoughts and feelings. You will see how it would be easier to have a professional guide you through it, but you can do it on your own.

Take 5 deep breaths, get settled, comfortable and relax. Continue to breathe deeply and ask your mind to bring up an activity, from any time in your life. Make sure it is an activity that you enjoyed and could perform well.

Now take however long you need to recall a specific time when you became naturally immersed in that activity and started performing at a personally brilliant level of skill.

Perhaps you were playing a sport and you became 'untouchable,' moving with game-winning grace, speed, strength and finesse ...

Or you were working on an assignment and your focus became so precise that all the puzzle pieces came together due to repeated moments of intellectual momentum-building insight...

Or you were conversing with someone at such a deep level of connection and understanding that it became a truly life enhancing experience ...

Choose just one experience when you were at your best, simply allow whatever memory is at the forefront of your mind to surface ...

And really notice what was going on as if it is happening again now.

Notice the way you look, breathe, move and feel.

Continue breathing deeply and immerse yourself in this experience ...

What do you feel now and where in your body is it strongest? Allow that feeling to radiate even more deeply inside of you.

What can you see? You have full control of the camera in your mind. Sharpen that image and make it even brighter, bigger and bolder.

What do you now hear? Choose just one sound, even if it is just the sound of your breath, the actual sound of silence or something more vibrant, make your chosen sound stronger, louder and fuller.

If there is anything you can smell or taste, absorb those sensations completely.

Now really experience everything you can see, hear, feel, taste and smell ...

Completely connect to that activity. Feel yourself flowing, as if you are one with it. Make a sound that represents how you feel.

Further intensify your level of immersion, your level of connectedness with that activity. Imagine a level to a gear box that has five ascending gears. Move to Gear 2 and brighten and fall deeper into the experience. See the colours, the light and the movement intensify. Feel the adrenaline begin to flow.

Gear 3. Stay immersed and connected. Enjoy it.

Gear 4. Freely make that sound again. Make the colours, light and movement even bigger, brighter, sharper and clearer. Fall deeper and deeper, where there is nothing else. Become one with that experience.

Gear 5. With full intensity you are completely at one with that experience. You are the experience, the color, the light, the movement, the sensation. Feel it entirely, let the experience flow perfectly through you.

And with each breath build it up towards a peak and just before the peak...

Double that feeling... and then double the whole feeling again and again.

Then imagine whatever related task you have that needs to be done and experience yourself completing every core part of it perfectly. Fully experience yourself actively solving all the key problems and fully enjoying the experience. Use your mental camera in a way that naturally promotes success.

Amplify what you want. Make objects and yourself and your expressions bigger, brighter louder and more pristine. Reduce the intensity of the difficult parts, make them smaller, or duller, or softer. Work through it until you have a feeling where all key elements have been solved, the task has been completed and you feel a true sense of achievement. Once you have done that ...

Take however long you like to fully absorb, enjoy and understand the experience and what you expect to achieve ...

Then let go of the imagery but take the feeling with you as you take five deep breaths, dropping down each gear, bringing a sense of refreshment, focus and energy into the moment now to be utilized for whatever activity that is to be done. Begin immediately if possible.

What about the Elephant? Panic, Choking and Mindful Acceptance

Sadly, even the greatest professionals in sports, business, sex and other life areas screw up performances. We tend to screw up either through "panic" which usually occurs due to a lack of preparation leading to catastrophic thinking or "choking" which occurs through over-thinking and over-analyzing.

Both are avoided through proper mental preparation. You avoid panic by knowing how to respond to emergencies. Practice calmly problem-solving emergency situations, just like a pilot does in a flight simulator. You circumvent choking by avoiding deep analysis of your behavior during a performance. You should set aside practice time to break up and analyze each aspect of a performance in order to improve it, but when actually performing, your focus must be on feeling your way through it.

Peak emotion and deep analysis cannot be achieved at the same time. The priming exercise is designed to help you create the right emotions and to feed off the unconscious skills you have already developed from previous successes. So, what do you do if catastrophic or overly analytic thoughts start to interfere with your performance?

You continue with your emotional priming and positive focus and mindfully accept and let go of catastrophic or analytical thoughts, gently continuing to re-focus on the desired emotions, expectations and actions. You must accept the elephant; do not push but rather dance with it. Feel and focus on what you do want, accept and let go of what you don't, and stick to rules of this perpetual cycle. Over time, your emotional and focus skills will grow and the influence of the elephant (relating to those unhelpful thoughts and feelings) will diminish. This will lead to longer and deeper peak performance flow experiences.

Principle Summary

Peak Performance: Demonstrate positive discipline and high self-confidence by regularly triggering and intensifying the right emotion on command.

Manipulate your mind and body in a way that allows you access to the "right" emotion before starting and to re-fire it during an important task. Prime yourself by re-experiencing a time in the past when you completed the same or a similar task in a way where you felt highly positive, productive and motivated and systematically amplify the feeling as required.

Fast-Action Techniques

1. When you create your peak performance scenarios, be ambitiously realistic but not entirely fanciful. Consider your current level of skill too. If you have never done a particular activity, you are not going to be amazing at it no matter how good your visualization. If you are currently feeling anxious or depressed, start with small and easy goals and build from there.
2. Consider three upcoming tasks. Write them down with a plan of how you will prompt yourself to be your best for each one. Be sure to also include how you will keep a strong focus and mindfully accept and adapt to any potential errors.
3. Study peak performing role-models. Examine and adopt elements of skill you see in others. It may be the physiology or technique of an athlete, great acting without sound to develop non-verbal perceptions, or interviews where role-models are discussing their mindset and preparation strategies. One video study method is to slow down and freeze frame movements and study them piece by piece, and practice each piece over and over until you can perform it smoothly as a whole. However, when it is time to perform, do not analyze, prime the right emotions and trust in your own mind and body.

Hypnotic Recording – Peak Performance Living: For guided assistance in moving beyond the principles and techniques of this chapter, a guided brain re-training process to assist you in priming and amplifying positive emotions so you can regularly trigger peak performance experiences and develop greater discipline and higher self-confidence in your personal and professional life is at http://mentalhealthhypnosis.com/peakperformances

Sensational Self Image
Construct new beliefs and emotions to strengthen identity, enhance self-esteem and build empowering belief systems

She is ugly and defective.

She spends almost all her waking hours (and some of her sleeping ones as well) obsessing over her appearance. Whatever she tries, nothing can hide her unsightliness. If only she was taller and thinner, especially around the waist. She can hide her knees, legs and feet, but not always her rough and bony hands. Then, of course, there is her face.

Eyes are too far apart, ears stick out, nose is crooked, teeth are stained, lips too thin, cheeks are droopy, forehead overly high and hair too frizzy. Make-up can only do so much!

Next stop – surgery.

Followed by – more surgery.

Then – a little more surgery and maybe a little more after that ...

He is dumb and dopey.

No matter how hard he tries, he always loses. He was only accepted into his third choice university. He foolishly chose not to study medicine and only completed a Masters but not a Doctorate. It took him six whole months to find a suitable position in his obscure profession after graduation. Nobody respects him or his profession. They know he is a fraud.

He needs to find a way to do more. If only he was quicker. If only he hadn't made all those stupid choices and did those higher courses. Just like his degree, he's practically useless!

Next stop – medical school.

Followed by – business school.

Then – law school ...

He thinks she is beautiful. She thinks he is intelligent. Neither love themselves or feels good enough for the other. She loves him and he loves her but they don't believe each other!

Before a major cosmetic surgery, patients are often advised to see a Psychologist. This is for two basic reasons. One is to see if a change on the outside will actually be accepted as a positive change on the inside (to their self-image). Secondly, will the surgery just lead to more imperfection seeking and obsessiveness, or will the change be appreciated and lead to greater overall happiness and life satisfaction?

Our true problems are rarely visible! Changing your face or having more diplomas on your wall will not change who you are. Only an internal adjustment can change who you are. Who you are is what you project. Like movie watching, it is not the canister that people look at, but what shines from it. What shines from it is based on how the film has been shot and organized inside of it.

Your self-image, how you view and refer to yourself, influences all your major life decisions. Although "Behavior is King," and continuing to act in a way that corresponds with your values and goals will lead to changes in your self-image, developing empowering beliefs about who you are makes it easier to feel good about yourself and the process of acting towards your values much easier.

Our Deepest Fears

To figure out our deepest fears, consider the babies in the orphanage from the chapter "Praise Pays." What was it that the children were starved of?

Physical expressions of ... love!

What would someone who receives little to no love from significant people conclude about themselves? That there must be something wrong with them, that they are "not good enough." All disempowering beliefs stem off these two—that "you're not good enough" and because you're not good enough, you won't be loved.

Failure, embarrassment, rejection, and so on, all these natural and inevitable painful experiences if not dealt with in an empowering fashion will lead to feelings of inadequacy or unworthiness (both relating to not being good enough) and to question whether you can be loved. It's true, not everyone receives as much love as they should, but that doesn't mean that difficult past experiences should have to dictate your present self-image and future possibilities.

Rules of empowerment

Harness Your Uniqueness: You are you. There is only one of you, and that is the source of your power. No one looks like you or can do what you can as a whole. As discussed in "Authentic Achievement" you have your own unique strengths and limitations. When you do utilize your strengths in the right way, no one can create what you can create. To do this you must ...

Seek Self-Acceptance: The ultimate confidence comes when you have nothing to hide. You do have physical imperfections and knowledge gaps. Self-esteem that is too low will limit you. If it is too high you run the risk of not valuing and avoiding the true effort required for success. To do this you must ...

Move beyond Labels: You are more than "good" or "bad." Those labels are far too simplistic. We've all made mistakes and we've all done wonderful things. Who you are depends not on the past, but what you are moving towards right now! If you are moving towards your values (not those of others) and progressing at the right speed for you (in acceptance of fears, doubts, and previous failures), then you are on the right path. When on the right path, you must ...

Praise Your Potential: Be curious, open and appreciative of what you discover. If you allow it, your own potential will surprise and humble you. It has happened to you many times in the past. Do not try to force progression, inspire it. Always seek lessons from positive and painful experiences. To do this you must ...

Decide what it will mean: Whether you face a positive or painful experience, the answer should always be the same. "How do I use this in an empowering way?" All scars and setbacks have a story and once accepted can be transformed into symbols of strength and greater purpose. To do that, it is important to re-frame difficult experiences in order to replace limiting beliefs.

Example Re-frames for Common Limiting Beliefs

1. **I'm not good enough**

You know what, you're right! You're not good enough. If you were, you would already have whatever it is you are working towards. The point is that no one is instantly successful. No one is good enough in the beginning. It's a process. Therefore, one way to directly challenge this belief is…

Re-frame: My competence grows with effortful practice.

2. **I don't deserve it (unworthy)**

Why not you? Why does some other chump deserve the win more than you do? The way I see it, everybody (except for the truly troubled and cruel) deserves a great life. Everybody deserves to win. Now of course, not everybody will, which means when you do get a win, it should be doubly celebrated. The trouble of course is guilt. Somewhere along the line you were taught others deserve more than you because they worked harder or are more disadvantaged or whatever. Rubbish! If they get a win, great, good on them. If you're smart, you'll pay attention to what they did so you can do better next time. If you get a win, even better, good on you! It's that simple.

Re-frame: Whether I win or not, I deserve success.

3. **I'm a failure**

If you were a failure, you'd be dead by now. As long as you're breathing and moving, there is only one way to fail and that is to stop trying to learn. Now it's actually pretty hard to stop learning. Considering we are designed to learn, you would actually have to interrupt your very nature in order to attempt to do so. The only sure-fire way to do that is to die. It's never about failure, but rather how you perceive the learning process.

Re-frame: I'm a learner (and a pretty darn stubborn one too).

4. I don't have the money/time/resources

Neither does that guy, or that girl, or that annoying 15-year-old kid tinkering in his or her parents' shed and on their way to becoming a multi-millionaire. It's never a question of money/time/resources but passion, perseverance and resourcefulness. There is always time if you want it bad enough and are patient. There is always a way to find more money/resources if you keep connecting to more and more people and are patient enough. The key is patience and perseverance. Both are essential traits.

Re-frame: I will consistently work at it and find the money/time/resources.

5. I'm going to get laughed at (embarrassed, rejected)

Yes, yes you are. If not laughed at, then you will be ridiculed in some other way. There is an a-hole in every bunch. However, also realize it's a lot rarer than you think. Most people, and hopefully that includes the ones closest to you are supportive. The question is what does it mean? The answer is what people say about others is much more a reflection of them than of the person they are referring to. In other words, being laughed at is more about them attempting to mask their own fears and inadequacies than yours.

Re-frame: The people that matter will appreciate and respect my efforts. I appreciate and respect my efforts.

6. I won't be able to maintain it if I am successful

This one's a doozy. Welcome to the strange world of self-sabotage. Self-sabotage is based on a real problem, being that maintaining and growing success takes more effort and sustainable growth than the initial achievements. It's hard work! So the critical part of you in its constant effort to protect you may try to get you to fail because it will be easier in one sense but of course disappointing in the grand scheme of things. The key here is to remember that you are deserving and you are built to learn. Otherwise you never would have succeeded in the first place.

Re-frame: The first time is the hardest. If I've done it once, I will be able to do it again and again …

7. **I could lose everything (large or small risks - emotional, social, financial, or physical)**

Too true. But then again, many things could happen to you. You could be struck by lightning or picked at random to win a prize. The next person you meet may become your best friend or someone who is trying to take advantage of you in some way. Who knows? I don't think it has to be about winning or losing, but rather a careful consideration of risk-to-reward. You take a risk every time you leave the house and sometimes by staying in it. What you really want to consider is "Do I want this and what is the smartest way to go about it?" My motto is: always follow your dreams but cover your responsibilities. Take as many calculated risks as you can but never risk more than you can afford to lose.

Re-frame: I will always seek a healthy balance between risk and reward and cover my responsibilities.

8. **I don't want to feel alone (especially if going against an influential person)**

I respect your honesty. The truth is, humans are social creatures, and the decision to go off and work on things (often by yourself) is a difficult one to make. However, by taking those sometimes lonely leaps of faith you get to finally learn how to rely on the most important person in your life. Yourself! You learn that you are more resilient than you thought and that you can cope. It's a crucial lesson that must be learnt. Self-reliance is an extremely attractive trait. Ironically, this also tends to improve your relationships because you become more appreciative and efficient with the time you do have with others, and of course, less in need of their approval.

<u>Re-frame: I will become comfortable with my own company and make the most of my time with others.</u>

Beliefs into Targeted Stories (Mind Movies)

Once you have your empowering re-frames, you can then safely work on further enhancing your self-image. As much as we enjoy language, sensory experiences are what drive us the most. Positive beliefs and language must be integrated with your imagination. This of course happens naturally, but we can amplify the process.

This is where you create your mind movies and imagine your best-self performing at your peak (see Peak Performance Principle) with full experiential power. You work to see, hear, feel, smell, taste, and positively focus on being at your best across a range of different experiences. This is very much what hypnotic brain re-training is based on.

You can go into your past with the lessons you now have and re-imagine and enhance a memory. You can amplify the present. However, what is often most useful is the targeting of important future events, problem solving and experiencing them as successes before they happen, thus becoming more prepared and creating a stronger and more realistic expectation of success.

The goal can be as simple as going for and enjoying a walk. It can be more complex such as doing well at a job interview or being charming at a social gathering and highly complex like finishing a massive long-term career or lifestyle project.

As you know by now, at times an unwanted "elephant" (thought or feeling) may pop up in your experience. Notice, accept, let go and re-focus on what you do want as often as you need to. As you continue practicing, your mind will surprise you by showing you another path beyond your previous limits. Then it simply becomes time to "act now."

Principle Summary

Sensational Self Image: Construct new beliefs and emotions to strengthen identity, enhance self-esteem and build empowering belief systems.

How you view and refer to yourself shapes your identity and influences all your major life decisions. You need to actively build empowering beliefs and "mind movies" of future success that reinforce your uniqueness and show how you are good enough and worthy of love.

Fast-Action Techniques

1. Reflect on the three most common things you say about yourself that could be seen as negative or disempowering. Create an empowering re-frame for each and write them down. Keep the written reframes in your wallet or on your phone and read over them regularly, especially if feeling negative or disempowered.
2. Look into a mirror, breathe deeply and imagine previous experiences of love, kindness and curiosity. As you look at yourself, repeat these sentences based on the rules of empowerment out loud. "I am unique, I accept myself, I am more than any label, I am worthy of love and my life is meaningful." Repeat daily for one week.
3. Practice creating mind movies (with amazing and empowering special effects) of yourself being at your best and problem solving important future challenges. Aim to experience success before the event occurs. As previously stated, *the goal can be as simple as going for and enjoying a walk. It can be more complex such as doing well at a job interview or being charming at a social gathering and highly complex like finishing a massive long-term career or lifestyle project.* If negative thoughts or beliefs occur, notice, accept, let go and refocus on your empowered re-frames and what you do want as often as you need to.

Hypnotic Recording – Sensational Self-Image: For guided assistance in moving beyond the principles and techniques of this chapter, a guided brain re-training process to assist you in strengthening positive identity, enhancing self-esteem and building empowering belief systems and success expectations is available now at – http://mentalhealthhypnosis.com/selfimage

Your Two Bonus Chapters

Congratulations on working through the 20 core principles of superior mental health. After going through everything I have ever created to date and reflecting on my clinical psychology career in order to uncover the core 20 principles, I realized there was still a couple of areas I should address. The 20 core principles are about developing yourself whilst these two bonus chapters are more focused on positively influencing others. Of course, by positively influencing others, your self-development will increase as well.

The two bonus chapters (I have been assisting people in these areas for years but have never written about them before) are on relationships and social skills. As important as it is to improve your own mind, none of us exist in a vacuum. Interacting well with others is essential for happy living. Most of us dream of having a fantastic relationship. Unfortunately, few people understand the core rules for maintaining one.

We also strive for positive social influence and acceptance as well as to know how to effectively deal with bullies and other negative people. Far too many people struggle in these key life areas. That is why I decided to include these two additional bonus chapters.

May you use the following principles to create friends, inspire lovers and charm bullies.

Bonus: Principles of Magnetism

Harmonious Relationships
Build positive and lasting relationships, communication and harmony

Before you know it, you feel it! Instinct always precedes conscious recognition. Your heart increases, your breath becomes shorter and your pupils dilate well before you realize who has suddenly enslaved your attention. Attraction is like a massive asteroid about to destroy your defences. It cannot be controlled, and it cannot be stopped until it meets its target and when it does only one thing is guaranteed. There is going to be a lot of debris. Usually when two opposing forces collide, they simply bounce off each other. However, every now and then, they drive into each other and lock in place. This is a relationship.

I've never been in a bad relationship! I am more proud of this than anything else I have ever experienced or achieved and yet I have never publicly talked about it before. Now that doesn't mean that there was never any hurt, frustration, sadness or tears. Oh believe you me, both I and the people I have had relationships with have shared plenty of that. The ending of a relationship is painful, this is an inescapable truth. There is always debris. The question is: Can it be properly contained?

Pain and loss is not bad. It is simply inevitable. When I say I have never been in a "bad relationship," what I mean is there was never any additional pain (of course, there were a lot of great times too). There were always certain rules and principles I have followed so as to not add fuel onto the fires of disagreement and loss either during or after a relationship.

Discounting the obviously terrible effects of physically abusive or verbally aggressive relationships, non-abusive relationship issues are still extremely common causes of anxiety and especially depression. A very high percentage of people struggling with anxiety or depression are dissatisfied with their intimate or other close relationships. Many people seem to hope medication will somehow solve their problems or those of their partner. Medication may assist in reducing stress and improving mood so there is less chance of conflict, but it cannot fix or improve a relationship.

It is very much the positive focus and praise principles that are essential to continuously developing the right kind of relationships. Review these chapters again if you need to and consider applications for friends, family and partners. A relationship is not about maintenance. It is a live entity and must be grown or it will start to die. You should be regularly connecting over shared interests, frequently verbally and non-verbally praising of each other and striving for more harmony and fun as opposed to fewer fights or less boredom.

How to Reduce Conflict by Increasing Harmonious Communication

There are really only two causes of relationship conflict. One is differences of opinion in terms of how things should be done (our rules) and the other is ineffective communication. In both cases, developing harmonious communication is essential.

Clarify the intention: Always seek clarification before jumping to conclusions in regards to anything that could be read in more than one way. Miscommunication is frequent in relationships. Aim to understand the intention of what they have said. The easiest way to do this is to ask in a curious tone – "When you said X, what specifically did you mean by that?"

Reduce accusations: Whenever possible, aim to use "we" and "us" as opposed to "you" and "I" in relation to solving problems. Finding solutions and improving is much more important than who is more at fault. Blame leads to increasing defensiveness and problem solving is virtually impossible when people are angry or defensive.

"You have been really argumentative lately and I don't like it. You need to stop it."

Compare to "I know we haven't been getting along very well lately. Both of us could be calmer. Any ideas about what we should do?"

Name calling is taboo: It is never okay to insult your partner's character. Only damage will be done and nothing will be solved. Like the previous example, avoid "I" and "you" when upset. Avoid "I think you are ... dumb, stupid, ugly, fat, a bitch, a loser, a jerk, useless, a no-hoper" etc.

Frequently use playful and positive labels and nicknames: Make sure both of you like the names and labels regularly used towards each other and they are completely positive. Use words like fun, cute, smart, and sexy as much as possible.

Offer elegant as opposed to raw truth: Except for in very rare circumstances where it may be important to say exactly how you feel (and even then you should still probably work to express yourself as elegantly as you can), aim to be as elegantly honest as possible. You only need to offer just enough honesty to solve the problem. Being too raw in your honesty is likely to cause defensiveness and reduce the chance of the problem being solved.

Your partner asks "How do I look?" You think, "Terrible."

Elegant answer: "That's fine, however I think those outfits over there would suit you better."

"I don't know why I failed?" You think "It's because you play too many games, pretend the test will be easy and don't manage your time."

Elegant answer: "I know you didn't get quite the result you wanted so let's look into how to do it better next time."

"I'm ugly" You think, "Stop being so insecure."

Elegant Answer: "I wouldn't be with you if that was true. (Add "you're beautiful" but only if you genuinely feel like saying it at the time). What could we/you do right now that would make you feel more attractive?"

Seek to understand and respect how the other deals with pain: You will not always have the same beliefs or coping mechanisms. Generally speaking, men tend to shut down and work on the problem themselves and women prefer to talk it out. These two coping styles are clearly incompatible if attempted at the same time. However, issues must be communicated if they are to be resolved. The secret is to be gentle in finding agreement for when they will be discussed. Give options! You must respect the style and time the other person may need before they are ready. Try not to leave more than a day before discussing an important issue.

If they want to talk and you are not ready to listen say: "I know you want to talk about this but I can't give you the attention you deserve at the moment. Can we speak after dinner or before work tomorrow?"

If they have emotionally shut down say: "It looks like you need some time to process this. I'll come back in half an hour and see how you're going. (After half an hour) Are you ready to talk yet or should we leave it until after dinner or tomorrow?"

Listening versus problem solving: Another common generality is that men like to quickly problem solve whilst women often prefer to talk out their problems in order to process them. It really does not matter either way. A person should be heard and empathised with first anyway and secondly encouraged to find their own solution before offering your own. A solution you come up with yourself is more likely to be accepted and acted on and leads to greater independence. You should aim to listen and guide the other person towards solving it themselves and only if necessary after this gently ask "Would you like to hear my thoughts?" If they say yes, make sure you present your solution as elegantly as possible.

Work to agree and to agree to disagree: Always seek compromise and empathic understanding of the other's point of view. It is best to try it both ways, modifying approaches together and seeing what works best. If compromise over a particular issue is not possible, clearly outline the specific conditions around what is likely to happen and the expected consequences so as to avoid later misunderstandings.

Disagreements and anger: Never send angry written communication, period! Especially, not after a disagreement or argument. You will now have a written record of something you will most probably regret having written 24 hours later and probably spark an aggressive back and forth exchange. Unless it is somehow an emergency, it can wait. Write it if you want but don't send it. Wait 24 hours before reviewing it again. If you still want to send any of it, aim to make it as elegant as possible first. This does not mean you should not be honest, you can mention being hurt or disappointed etc., but avoid name calling and potentially unfair accusations.

You must respect the time out rule: Make an agreement that if either of you can feel yourself getting too angry or overwhelmed, you can call for a time out and the other person must do their best to leave the issue and the person alone for at least half an hour and not return to discussing it until both people are calm enough to do so. Of course, the actual problem or the immediately solvable elements of it should still be resolved if possible within a day.

Focus on the positive as much as possible: Don't forget to offer regular praise, seek harmony and growth and schedule in fun activities together. Ensure you commit to doing and maintaining those activities together. It is extremely important!

Celebrate positive life choices and directions: This is the biggest key to harmonious relationship longevity. Praise your partner's achievements and actively enjoy discussing how those achievements are likely to lead to a better life for you both.

*** Communicating with children during separation: Unfortunately sometimes relationships do not work out. Aim to never badmouth your partner in front of the children even if they are doing it to you. Deflect poor behaviour and regularly reassure the child. Often say something like "Sometimes when people are upset, including adults, they might say mean and nasty things. Your other parent and I will have to learn to be nicer to each other. Know that I (use "we" only if you believe it to be true) will always love you and do the best I can to help you."

Accepting Uncertainty

There are certain truths that you must accept. Your partner will think about others sexually and it is highly possible that they could be happy with someone else. That of course does not mean that is what they want, only that it's possible. There must be a foundation of trust or it just won't work. Harmonious communication is the best way to build trust, but of course, there are no guarantees. Many people struggle to accept the uncertainty that comes with a relationship and so work to control their partner.

The more you try and control your partner, the greater the chance you will have of losing them. Even if you do not lose them physically, you will lose them emotionally. They will resent you and they will stray, if not physically, then emotionally. They will start developing deeper connections with others, quite possibly just one other, and even less of one with you.

Love is a continuous leap of faith. If both follow the guidelines outlined in this section, your love should only grow over time. Although the signs are usually pretty obvious for a partner being unhappy and therefore on the path to eventual break up, sometimes both people do everything right and it still just doesn't work out. I guarantee you nothing!

The reason why my previous relationships didn't work out was because we discovered our values and goals were too different. Sometimes the asteroids need to unlock and go their separate ways with hopefully not too much debris. At the time of writing, I have been in my current relationship for 12 years. Our bond appears stronger than ever but I am no fool! Although I am confident and expectant of continued happiness together, I accept that our values could change one day and it could end. Of course, it is not what I focus on, but I accept the possibility.

For the first five years of our relationship we lived on opposite sides of the world. We really only had two choices. Trust each other or end it. Based on this experience, I can offer you one final piece of relationship advice. You are more than your relationship and your life must remain full and meaningful whether you have a partner or not. Our goal was to always strive to be complete and happy people even when we were not together. A relationship must be seen as a gift, as the icing on the cake, not the cake itself. That other person is not your only reason to live. Relationships amplify life experiences, both positive and negative. They amplify the pleasure and the pain. You must focus on and build the positives but also mindfully accept the uncertainties of life and of love.

Principle Summary

Harmonious Relationships: Build positive and lasting relationships, communication and harmony.

Regularly connect over shared interests, praise often and strive for harmonious communication. Seek to clarify, listen with empathy and patience and respect the different ways and the time your partner needs (within reason) to deal with pain. Use positive labels, communicate the truth elegantly and celebrate each other's positive life choices and directions.

Fast-Action Techniques

1. Remember that you are more than your relationship (with your partner, friend, family member etc.) and can still be happy without them. This will give you the freedom to create a better and deeper connection. Work to accept the pleasure and the pain involved in relationships and find the lessons in both. *If for any reason you feel you are in an abusive relationship, seek professional assistance.*
2. Work to implement elegant communication as often as possible. Keep asking yourself "How can I speak with more … kindness, charm, fun, elegance, positivity" and so on.
3. Reflect on some recent successes that your partner has experienced (they do not have to be large either (e.g. starting a new hobby, exercising more or something related to work or family etc.), and praise them. Show that you are proud and discuss how these successes could lead to the betterment of both of your lives. Do this regularly, it is most important.

Hypnotic Recording – Relationship Love, Fun and Harmony: For guided assistance in moving beyond the principles and techniques of this chapter, a guided brain re-training process to assist you in becoming more actively loving, patient, harmonious, positively communicative, sexy and fun in relation to your partner is available at – http://mentalhealthhypnosis.com/relationship

Superior Social Skills
Unleash social confidence, increase leadership status, become more attractive and charm workplace bullying bosses

You see him or her from across the room and you just know. You feel it! There is something about that person. They have an energy, deeply alluring and totally intoxicating. Surrounded by smiles, the social leader captures them every time. The listeners are transfixed, pleasantly afloat in a social trance.

As you watch from your distant corner you suddenly see an opening, the group has parted and you take a step forward but then realize "I have nothing to say!" Or, perhaps it's "I may say the wrong thing" and of course there is "What if they reject me?" You then take two steps back to make sure you're safe! You breathe a sigh of relief. Unfortunately the next breath is of disappointment. You let it go, again! That opportunity to connect is gone, perhaps forever.

We've all been there. We have all let thousands of opportunities to connect slip past us. On the flip side, some of the best experiences in our life will come from when we take that chance. Of course, feelings of anxiety and depression can interfere with our social confidence. When people are emotionally struggling, they tend to withdraw due to fear of rejection. Ironically, this is when the company of others can serve them the most.

Rejection Proofing: The Secret to Social Confidence

In an interaction, whether it is one on one, or in a group, whoever displays the strongest emotion is leading the interaction at that point in time and influences the emotions of all the other people involved. For example, in a two person interaction, if one person is showing deep sadness and the other person is moderately joyful, the sad person will have greater influence over the interaction at least in the beginning and will bring the emotion of the joyful person down towards sadness. The emotional reverse is also true.

Feeling sad is not necessarily a bad thing. By coming down to the sadder person's emotion, the joyful person has a better opportunity to understand and empathise with him or her. By feeling understood, the sad person is likely to begin to feel better and as the sad person begins to feel better the joyful person may then choose to take the lead and bring the sad person up towards a more positive feeling. However, the assumption here is that you would really only do this with a friend in need of comfort and understanding, and this chapter is more focused on positive social connection and charm.

Humans are social creatures and the more positive our social interactions the better we feel. In our brain, we have mirror neurons and basically what they are there to do is help us tune into and copy the emotion of someone else so we can better understand them. As we do that we loop with each other's emotion and the emotion builds in intensity. So, the happier they feel, the happier we begin to feel, and then as we begin to feel happier they start to feel even happier and then so do we and on it goes. People will mirror each other through gesture, posture and facial expression physically and the same occurs internally as more and more mirror neurons go to the same parts of each individual's brain.

Social Influence is a Choice

Often the person who naturally demonstrates stronger emotion and therefore higher influence over others is the person with the higher social status position. This is because a social expectation is created. For example, a manager in a workplace has a higher status position than the workers. Often the emotion the manager brings will influence the staff. If the manager is angry and irritable, it is likely that the entire staff will suffer in how they feel. Alternatively, if the manager is joyful and in a positive mood, it is likely that the staff as a whole will experience an increase in mood and productivity.

However, it is not your social status position but the strength and selection of the emotional frameworks you choose to generate that will determine your own mood and how you influence others.

Even if your supervisor was angry or stressed, it does not have to influence your mood if in an interaction with him or her you displayed an even stronger level of calm or excitement. In this case you would be likely to influence him or her and reduce the intensity of their emotion even though they have the higher position.

Unfortunately though, this is rare, as most people unconsciously attune to the emotion of the person with the higher preordained status, rather than deciding to empathise with the person if it is possible and lead them to a more positive emotion. At any point in an interaction, you're either leading or being led.

Positivity Creates Real Attractiveness

Positive emotional expression and selection is the key to attractiveness. Whether social or intimate, it is always the culmination of the emotions you generate that are more influential than your physical appearance. The emotions you spend the majority of your time living in will be the most influential factor in regards to how socially and physically attractive you are to yourself and other people. No matter how physically attractive someone is, if they consistently over time display strong negative emotions, they will become less attractive to other people.

The research into happiness has consistently found that one of the strongest predictors of happiness in people is having a fun, social and outgoing nature. This is what psychologists call being extroverted and gregarious. One reason for this is because we loop onto each other's emotions and by bringing a positive attitude to a social encounter, it will then be enhanced and amplified by other people's happier reactions to you. As the conversation continues, the positive emotions continue to be amplified and thus over time shaping and strengthening more positive emotion and mood.

Simplifying Positive Social Connection

Time to outline the social skills process. The key is you must take emotional leadership and regularly guide the emotional direction of the interaction. Therefore it is best to be emotionally primed before you even begin socializing.

Beforehand preparation: Put yourself in a strong positive emotional state. You want to work with feelings like warmth, openness, fun, or whatever you assume to be most appropriate for the situation. Whatever you want them to feel is what you must feel first.

Review **peak performance** if you need to refresh on how to do this.

Brief interesting and positive story creation: This is optional but highly useful in guiding people towards fun, interesting and positive topics. It helps if your short story is related to the context you are in but it does not have to be. Below are a few examples. With all of these stories, I could elaborate for considerably longer if I wanted which would set the emotional tone more.

At a dinner party: Food here smells great. I once had Pizza in Venice; it was great to have such tasty food and in such a beautiful setting. What's your favourite food? (Or - Where is the best place you've ever had a meal?)

Job networking: All these different professions make me think back to simpler times. I started out mowing lawns and recycling cans for a few bucks an hour. I'd come home with all sorts of grazes and in need of an immediate shower. Still it was great to have my own money. What was your first job? What was the best part of it and what are you glad you left behind?

Stranger in the park (perhaps with a dog): My friend has the silliest dog! Lovable, cute and very sneaky. The other day his dog buried his TV remote for the fifth time. We all say my friend watches too much TV anyway. Do you have (any) other pets?

Focus on Positive Terms and Topics

Terms: Ask about their favorite or best or most interesting or funniest or weirdest etc.

Topics: Travel, pets, parties, movies, music, hobbies, gifts, food, where they are from

Generally avoid: Weather, work (both often boring), religion, politics (both controversial)

Before the meeting: Complete a short mind movie of the social encounter going well.

During the Social Encounter

1. Offer a large warm smile and open body posture as soon as you see them. Do not hesitate! This way you take immediate emotional leadership. Offer a handshake if warranted and simply say "hi" or something to that effect.
2. (Optional) Casually and curiously praise them. E.g. "Hey cool watch, great color. I like the bigger numbers."
3. Tell your context related story to set the scene then ask them a context related question. E.g. About a watch or the current situation.
4. Go back and forth between telling positive stories and aspects of yourself and most importantly asking them about positive aspects of their life.
5. (Essential) Always keep the conversation fun and positive. Empathise with any negative comments and immediately re-direct to the positive.

Below are **highly unlikely** negative responses. It does not matter how negative a response is – keep redirecting to the positive.

"It's a shame you hate your job. What would you love to do?"

"It is sad when a pet dies. What's been your best experience with an animal?"

"Talking to a stranger can feel weird. When have you had a good experience talking to a stranger? After all, your closest friends would have been strangers once."

"I can see why you don't like your hometown. Where do you wish you were raised? (They answer.) Why there? What's good about that place?

6. Leave as soon as conversation starts to come off its peak. Don't let it die, even if it was very short. Say something like "Great to meet/see you. I better head off. Hope to catch you again soon."

Charming Bullies

Bullying is a massive problem and a huge cause of mental health issues. Unfortunately, many people have to deal with bullies and often the bully is in a very high status position like their boss. One option is to be more assertive towards the bully, however this can lead to a lot of conflict and be more trouble than it's worth. I prefer whenever possible (assuming reporting the bullying is futile) to help people charm their way past bullies, especially in work contexts. Of course, the principles of the strategies outlined above will also work with bullies too in situations where they are not bullying you.

In bullying situations, the secret is to be calm and **agreeable without agreeing**. This way you keep your dignity and you admit to nothing whilst the bully feels like they are being heard, understood and respected. Always accurately document all bullying interactions in case you need to refer to them later.

There are three things you want to do. Empathise (E) with their intention, ask (A) for specific proof of what you have been accused of and say how you will solve (S) the problem even if there is no proof.

1. False accusation by bully: You're always late.

Response: (E) It is important that we all do our fair share and set a good example. I was 19 minutes late today but I also worked 35 minutes longer than usual yesterday. However, it is important to be on time. (A)Do you have any other specific examples of me being late?

Bully: Yes, but I don't have the exact dates on me.

Response: Okay, well, I can't recall any. I'd have to check my diary too, but if you come across them, please bring them to my attention. (S) Either way, it is important to get in on time and that is always what I am aiming to do.

2. False accusation by bully: You have badmouthed or spread gossip about someone.

Response: (E) Hurting someone's feelings is definitely not and would never be my intention. (A) Can you tell me more about the accusation?

Bully: I can't, it's confidential at this time.

Response: Well, I am unaware of anything I would have said that could be offensive. (S) Regardless, I'll be sure to be more careful and even more positive than usual in the future.

3. False accusation by bully: You did it wrong.

Response: (E) Clearly there has been a mistake and of course we want to avoid them and provide a professional service. (A) As far as I know I followed the precise instructions given to me in the original email. There was a second email which had some inconsistencies with the instructions of the first email and I did seek written clarification on date X and Y but did not get a response. Since the deadline was approaching, I went off the original. (S) However, in the future, I'll aim to run it by you in person if you think it will help.

In all of these examples, there is not really much more the bully can say because you've already committed to solving the problem. This should make such irritating confrontations as short as possible and reduce the frequency of accusations. Combined with regular use of the positive social skills techniques, it is highly possible to change their attitude towards you in a short period of time. As you can see from all the examples, always display a desire to solve problems (even if they are based on false accusations) and work to empathise but never apologize unless you actually did do something wrong.

Principle Summary

Superior Social Skills: Unleash social confidence, increasing leadership status, becoming more attractive and charming workplace bullying bosses.

Whoever displays the strongest emotion will lead the interaction and have the highest influence no matter their status. Strong positive emotion is the key to attractiveness and use positive story topics and re-direction when meeting others. Be agreeable without agreeing and problem solving focused in order to charm bullies.

Fast-Action Techniques

1. Consider three upcoming situations. Make sure to be emotionally primed and prepared. As soon as you see them, immediately present positively and aim to take emotional leadership. Have your short stories prepared if you like and just dive in. If you get stuck, say 'great to see you' and leave.
2. The most important emotion in conversation is curiosity. Be curious when speaking to others and focus more on the emotion they are presenting rather than what they are saying. If they start speaking about a negative topic, immediately empathise and re-direct towards a positive topic.
3. Make an effort to influence people you would prefer to avoid. Aim to have a conversation with this kind of person at least 1-2 times a week. Use skills previously outlined to practice charming pessimists, bullies or other negative or boring people in your life. Also practice positively connecting to 1-2 strangers a week.

Hypnotic Recording – Superior Social Skills: For guided assistance in moving beyond the principles and techniques of this chapter, a guided brain re-training process to assist you in making a great first impression, increasing social attractiveness and confidence and positively connecting to others with greater ease is at – http://mentalhealthhypnosis.com/superiorsocialskills

Medication

Medication is a personal choice for someone who may be struggling with anxiety or depression. However, medication is heavily overprescribed and carries a range of associated lifestyle and health risks that should not be ignored.

As a general rule, someone with mild to moderate level symptoms should seek therapeutic intervention first as medication is often unnecessary for people at this symptom level. If at the severe to extremely severe level, therapeutic intervention should be sought and medication is to be seriously considered.

The issue with medication is of course side effects and potential over-reliance. Some of the most challenging antidepressant side-effects that may occur are mental fogginess, nausea, an inability to feel high level positive emotion like excitement and reductions in sex drive. If warranted, medication should be viewed as a short to medium term intervention.

Ideally, it should be seen the way a cast is used for a broken leg. Medication can help create a more mentally stable environment. The reduction in fluctuations in mood, especially negative mood, can allow the person to feel more secure and better able to focus on developing the life skills they should be building through psychological training and/or therapy. As the person heals and grows (not unlike the bone of a broken leg), medication should be reduced (under correct medical supervision) and eventually removed.

There are situations where long term medication use may be warranted, but this should be the exception rather than the expectation. Unfortunately, due to the over-prescription of medication, too many extended term users should have ceased usage long ago and may unnecessarily develop dependency issues.

Depression and antidepressants: Antidepressants are generally not physically addictive. Long term use may reduce a person's confidence in feeling able to cope in life without them. Trial and error may also be required in order to find the most suitable one. Sometimes the wrong antidepressant can make someone feel worse, or even suicidal, so it is very important to be in regular contact with your medical provider and to see them immediately if you are reacting poorly to the medication.

Anxiety and anti-anxiety medication: Anti-anxiety medication (e.g. benzodiazepines) are often highly physically addictive. Occasional use to assist in high anxiety situations is generally okay. However, from a psychological point of view, using anti-anxiety medication prevents a full natural exposure and potential habituation to the fear. Therefore, it will only prevent the feeling of anxiety but will not help you overcome the cause of it.

Sleeping tablets: Occasional use is generally okay. Regular use is to be avoided as most are highly addictive and prolonged use can interfere with natural sleep patterns.

Pain killers: These can be highly addictive. It is important to seek other interventions in addition to medication for chronic pain issues.

Anti-psychotics and others: Anti-psychotics and other uncommon psychiatric medication use is rare and should only be prescribed by professionals with special training on those medications and only to people with severely elevated mental illness issues.

In my opinion, unless the symptoms are severe or worse, it is best to use psychological and hypnotic interventions first before considering the addition of medication based assistance. Being on medication as a general rule will not interfere with psychological and hypnotic assistance. Never suddenly stop medication without having first discussed it with your doctor. You may need to be weaned off it. If unsure about what you feel is best, you can always seek a second medical opinion.

Dealing with Extreme Situations
Panic and Suicidality

If you or someone close to you is ever to go through an extreme period of anxiety or depression, it is vital that you know what to do. Extreme depression would be suicidality whilst an extreme episode of anxiety would be a panic attack. Common panic symptoms include shortness of breath, sweatiness, shaking, increased heart rate, churning stomach and catastrophic thinking. A panic attack sufferer will often think they could be dying.

Unfortunately, many panic symptoms resemble that of a heart attack. The first time someone has a panic attack, they may think it is a heart attack. If unsure, go to the hospital emergency room. However, your response should still be the same. Get them to focus on breathing deeply and speak in a soothing and re-assuring tone. Tell them they are safe, they are not going to die and the symptoms will pass. If in doubt that it could be more than panic, proceed with going to hospital emergency.

Immediate intervention is warranted if you or someone you know is suicidal. Take them to their family doctor, or call your local mental health team. If risk of suicide is imminent, take them to hospital emergency. It is important to distinguish between suicidal ideation, intention and plan. Ideation means they only have thoughts of suicide. It is important that close family or friends call or visit regularly to check in on the person during the period of them seeking professional help.

If someone says they actually intend to commit suicide, ask them if they have an actual plan of how and when they would do it. If they do not, still take them to their family doctor, organize a mental health team, visit or take them to emergency. If they do have a plan, remove all dangerous objects and be extra careful to not leave them alone at any time until professional assistance is obtained. If they have a plan, immediately organize a mental health team visit as you stay with them or, if not possible, take them to hospital emergency and stay with them until doctors advise otherwise. No matter what the suicidal person says, aim to be reassuring but also firm in terms of stating what you have to do and keep them in your line of sight at all times until the professionals have taken over.

Seeking Professional Assistance

Fortunately, nowadays there is less of a stigma on seeking mental health assistance. The reality is that we live in very stressful times and most of us are not raised or trained in knowing how to deal with the pressures of life.

I have put into this book what I truly believe to be the core principles of good mental health and the essentials for overcoming depression, anxiety and other related issues. However, as I said in the introduction, a book can only do so much. For someone who is more self-improvement focused or who is suffering from mild to moderate range issues (you can gauge this by testing yourself with the DASS21), the application of these principles alone can and often is enough to overcome a range of mental health issues. I have also provided links to additional hypnotic interventions (which tend to be faster and more thorough as I can guide you better with my voice) if seeking additional assistance in relation to a certain area of life. I believe these principles in combination with hypnotic re-training can and have created some fantastic results for the people I've counselled.

If you are in the severe or extremely severe range, all of these psychological and hypnotic interventions still apply and do assist, however it may be wise to seek additional assistance. Sometimes we need an in-person guide to help us through a difficult time. If you are struggling with severe to extremely severe anxiety or depression symptoms and have been struggling to apply what you have learnt in this book, see you family doctor to be assessed. If appropriate, you should be referred to a Clinical Psychologist or possibly a psychiatrist.

You are always welcome to email me at the email address aleks@fulfillinghappiness.com if you have a question. **DO NOT CONTACT ME IF IT IS AN EMERGENCY!** I cannot provide an answer to a complex psychological problem via email but I may be able to point you in the right direction. Although I do offer success and happiness coaching and may on special occasion offer assistance to someone with mild to moderate severity issues over the internet, I do not work online with someone in the severe range or higher as I believe it is extremely important to receive in-person one on one contact in those cases.

If you wish to see where I currently provide one-on-one coaching and therapy, visit the contact page on my main website http://FulfillingHappiness.com/contact It will say on the page where I am currently physically practicing, or if not, simply email me.

To put it simply, when in doubt, visit your family doctor and go from there. It never hurts to be aware of your options. Take care of yourself; after all there is only one you!

May you continue maximizing your mental health,

Aleks

Personal Bibliography and Research References

Thank you for reading Maximum Mental Health. My objective with this book is for your experience to feel like a coaching session where you spend minimal time reading and the majority of your time applying. If you liked what you read, I would appreciate your support.

Please take a moment to leave a review of this book on Amazon. I value your feedback and it helps me to continue writing the kind of books that people want.

Help me to help you by helping me to help you with your review :) Go to:

http://www.amazon.com/Aleks-Srbinoski/e/B005JWGWWY/

To be informed of upcoming books and projects, visit

MaximumMentalHealth.com and join the mailing list.

To review any of the supporting hypnotic recordings, visit

MentalHealthHypnosis.com

As mentioned in the introduction, I have gone through all my materials in order to create this book. Many elements I have only trained clients in, and have never written about before. Some sections of Maximum Mental Health were modified chapters from previous books. Links to all previous books are below.

Amazon Store: To view my author profile and the most up to date listing of my books:

http://www.amazon.com/Aleks-Srbinoski/e/B005JWGWWY/

Other Kindle Ebooks by Aleks:

- Happiness Up Stress Down: Increase Happiness and Decrease Stress in just 2 Minutes a Day over 2 Weeks and Help your Community (Happiness, Stress Management and Goal Setting, Volume 1)**

- Destiny Defining Decisions: Best-Selling Entrepreneurs Reveal their Greatest Success Secrets (Entrepreneur Interview Series)**

- Motivation Now: Productivity and Persuasion Secrets For Modern Day Excellence and Effectiveness (60 Minute Success Series)

- Instant Inner Calm: Simple Stress Management Strategies To Increase Clarity, Creativity and Calm (60 Minute Success Series)

- Precision Language: Powerful and Precise Positive Thinking Secrets For Personal and Professional Success (60 Minute Success Series)

- The 7 Mental Viruses Crushing Your Potential: Overcome Fear and Negative Thinking by Building a New Positive Mindset (60 Minute Success Series)

- 10 Life Success Secrets Revealed: Your Simple Guide To Success, Wealth and Fulfilling Happiness (60 Minute Success Series)

**Also available in print.

THE MENTAL HEALTH AND HAPPINESS SERIES

This is the first book in the Mental Health and Happiness series. Based on the feedback I receive, I hope to release more Mental Health enhancing books in the future.

References

A great deal of research went into the creation of this book. For a full list of references, visit:
MaximumMentalHealth.com/references

Special Acknowledgements

Thank you to all preliminary reviewers, supporters and those who offered praise for the book.

How to work with Aleks

Aleks George Srbinoski is an author, speaker and multidisciplinary psychologist focusing on mental health, success, happiness, entrepreneurship and numerous other self-improvement topics.

Known as a leading expert in success and happiness strategies, he is the founder of FulfillingHappiness.com and author of the Success Secrets Series, and the Fulfilling Happiness Program. Join his mailing list or use handle @AleksPsych to follow on twitter for updates.

He consults in person but also works with organizations and schools from all over the world through online training programs. Contact him via aleks@fulfillinghappiness.com to discuss how he may be able to assist you or your organization.